77 TALKS FOR BORED-AGAIN TEENAGERS

77 talks for Bored-Again Teenagers

Steve Maltz

MonarcH
BOOKS

Mill Hill, London & Grand Rapids, Michigan

First published by Monarch Books in the UK 2003,
Concorde House, Grenville Place,
Mill Hill, London, NW7 3SA.

Distributed by:
UK: STL, PO Box 300, Kingstown Broadway, Carlisle,
Cumbria CA3 0QS;
USA: Kregel Publications, PO Box 2607
Grand Rapids, Michigan 49501.

ISBN 1 85424 587 2 (UK)
ISBN 0 8254 6226 6 (USA)

British Library Cataloguing Data
A catalogue record for this book is available
from the British Library

Book design and production for the publishers by
Bookprint Creative Services
P.O. Box 827, BN21 3YJ, England.
Printed in Great Britain

Contents

Acknowledgements

First and foremost I would thank Monica, my wife and rock who earths and supports and sustains me when I veer off on my flights of fancy. Also my sons, Philip, Simon and Jony, for inspiration and criticism in equal measure. My mum for her creative genes and my dad for the constant loans. My sister Mish, Norma at CLC, and Steve and John at Monarch CCP for comments on early manuscripts. Last and not least, Tony at Monarch Books, for (finally) taking a chance on me and unleashing me on an unsuspecting world.

Introduction

What a task! It's not easy to compile a series of talks that are going to be equally relevant to big kids and young adults. You are looking at an age group ranging from those just getting to grips with secondary education, right through to "been-there-done-that" university undergraduates. But this shouldn't be an impossible task, as the Christian message is basically a simple one. It's just up to us to communicate that fact!

With teenage attention spans decreasing as fast as new channels appear on satellite TV, it's not just a case of presenting the gospel as it stands and hoping they "get it". In this post-modern age you have to hit them in bite-sized chunks to make an impact and make tentative steps into their world, rather than screaming through a loud hailer over the generation gap. "Make it interesting, make it exciting, make it interactive" is the cry. "It's the only way you're going to grab their attention." This series of talks is a first step along that rocky road and I pray that we can receive a similar response to Paul, when he encountered the Athenians, "You are bringing some strange ideas to our ears, and we want to know what they mean" (Acts 17:20).

Not all the talks in this book are going to "hit the spot" for your particular youth group, but if we can make an impact with some of them then we could make a difference in the lives of a sadly neglected but crucial segment of our population:

teenagers, the adults of tomorrow. The intention of this book is to provide solid foundational teaching on key topics, from the influence of the media to the Last Supper. There is a particularly thorough presentation of the gospel in the "Pastures Green" section, lasting eight weeks, though briefer versions, covering one and two weeks, are also included for those without the patience. Other topics include morality, self-worth, the Bible, abortion, Harry Potter, the Trinity, evolution, the crucifixion, the big bang, the deadly sins and euthanasia.

The book is divided into seven sections, arranged as colours of the rainbow. These sections represent seven checkpoints on our spiritual journey:

SIMPLY RED section – "Stir it up" – for groups who are reluctant, cynical and "didn't realise there was going to be a boring old talk". Our objective here is to intrigue and provoke and to open up the possibility of a life beyond what they can see, hear and feel.

TANGY ORANGE section – "Questions" – for groups who like a challenge and are reasonably open-minded, but nevertheless may only be prepared to give you one chance to impress. Our objective here is to introduce a spiritual element to life, with a gentle introduction to the Christian message.

MELLOW YELLOW section – "Answers" – for groups who are taking the bait and are willing to listen patiently, though it will still be possible to lose them if you are not relevant enough. Our objective here is to begin to answer key questions from a Christian perspective.

PASTURES GREEN section – "The gospel" – for groups ready to hear the Christian gospel in a culturally relevant and sensitive way. Our objective is to provide a clear and systematic introduction to the gospel, sufficient for them to respond with an informed decision for Christ.

MOODY BLUE section – "Assurances" – for groups largely made up of new Christians. Our objective is to provide them with a series of assurances and faith-builders to enable them to grow steadily.

INKY INDIGO section – "Blueprints" – for groups of new Christians who are becoming established in their faith. Our objective is to give them a series of guidelines to help them cope with the pressures of being Christians in a hostile world.

PARMA VIOLET section – "Solid food" – for groups of new Christians ready to move on in their faith and feed their minds. Our objective is to provide solid Bible teaching in key areas to help them to develop eager questioning minds.

Imagine you have been invited to a posh buffet. The selection of food is extensive, catering for all possible tastes and moods. The buffet is ongoing, with food continually topped up, and people come and go as they please, nibbling or pigging out, depending on their appetite. This book perhaps should be viewed in the same way. Although you could gorge yourself, by working systematically through the book, taking your youth group through all 77 talks, this would not be a good idea, as this means they won't be exposed to the gospel for at least eight months!

Instead I suggest you decide from day one where your group is currently "at" and start at the corresponding section of this book, depending on the degree of spiritual hunger. From there you can move at your own rate, selecting talks relevant to the interests and capabilities of your group. Some will have to be fed on a "light diet", others may want something to chew on. There's plenty here to suit all tastes!

Every talk includes sufficient material for a session lasting from fifteen minutes to an hour. I have also provided extra information, such as graphics, links and background reading, at the book website (www.77talksforteens.com) for you to download if necessary. The website also contains a discussion forum, so that you can share your successes (and failures!) and help each other to be more effective in communicating with teenagers.

So dive in and enjoy. My prayer is that you will be as blessed by using these talks as I was in writing them!

How to Use This Book

Here are some guidelines to help you get the most out of the material in this book.

Each talk includes:

- **THEME**: this is your introduction to what is being covered, and the objective of the talk
- **PREPARATION**: check here beforehand for material you'll need for the talk.
- **PRESENTATION**: this describes what to do and say.

Some talks in the first three sections also include:

- **PARTING SHOT**: a few provocative thoughts to leave them with.

Notations used in the presentations:

- *Italics* represent things to do, rather than things to say. Everything that you say is identified by ordinary type or **bold type** when stressing a point.
- **Q:** and **A:** signifies a short "Question and Answer" section. Encourage the group to answer questions, though answers are given to prompt discussions.
- **DISCUSSION** signifies where you can open up a discussion. I recommend that you do some background

reading (links to material are given on the website). Although pointers are given to prompt discussions, it is up to you to decide on the depth and breadth, from your knowledge of your youth group.

- **CHALLENGE:** these are optional challenges for people to think about over the forthcoming week. Remember to follow them up in the next session.

Length of session

On average each talk should last 15–30 minutes. An open-ended element is the time set aside for discussions of the material. It is up to you, with your knowledge of your audience, to decide how much time – and what depth – is needed for this activity. Also, if time is limited, be prepared for a session to be split up into two or three separate periods. Good times for these splits would be the periods set aside for discussions encouraging group members to think hard about the material and perhaps continuing the discussion in the next session.

Content of session

Ideally you'll be able to use the lesson material presented here exactly as written, but there may be situations where you need to bring out the pruning shears. No one knows your audience better than you, so do customise the material accordingly. Due to the rapidly changing vocabulary of our youth culture, I have tended to stick to neutral language that is likely to endure, rather than popular jargon. Feel free to modify the language used so that it fits your own particular style of delivery and audience. If you have stories from your own experience that can liven things up, then use them. You may also need to cut back on material to fit into a shorter time-frame, though you must be careful not to lose the thread of any carefully developed arguments.

Where there is a lot of material to plough through, I have structured the talks so that the audience can share in the burden (or joy?) of reading out sections aloud. This is a flexible feature and you may prefer to take on this burden yourself, or share it with fellow leaders, if you feel your audience is unwilling or unable to participate in this activity.

We would be interested to hear of your experiences and you are free to log on to our discussion forum on the Web at www.77talksforteens.com/discuss to share such experiences and help each other to become more effective in presenting the material.

SIMPLY RED SECTION

Stir It Up

1
One Moment in Time

Theme

An appreciation of history through examining historical artifacts, followed by a discussion about how we too have a past, present and future. The object is to show the futility of "living for the present" and to help us cope better with the future.

Preparation

The previous week encourage as many as possible to bring in objects, such as family heirlooms, that have a history (and where they are willing to speak about them). Get others to bring a photograph of themselves when they were a baby or a small child. Collect these photographs before the beginning of the session. OHP/flip chart to illustrate points.

Presentation

Has anyone brought in anything for our "show and tell", to coin a corny phrase?

(Encourage them to speak about the personal and family significance of what they have brought in. Make this section last no longer than five minutes, but make sure that everyone who wishes to, has a chance to speak. In case no one brings anything in, have an object or two of your own and be prepared to speak about them.)

Isn't it incredible to be able to look at things that **existed before you did**?

And which were (probably) made at the hands of someone who doesn't exist any more?

Believe it or not – the world existed before you did!

It's not such a weird thought – some people called **existentialists** *(write on chart)* believe that the only thing that they can be sure about is that they, themselves, exist and as for the rest of the world . . . *(shrug shoulders)*

So let's first clear this up – touch the person next to you, just to make sure they really exist, then we can move on.

Now we don't just exist in the present. Like the objects we examined, we, too, have a past. And I'm going to prove it.

(Show the photographs and get them to guess who is who.)

Isn't it amazing that these cute kids have become such . . . fine specimens of humanity?

But think of this . . . one day you'll be showing photos of how you are now to your grandkids, showing them what . . . fine specimens of humanity you were!

Yes . . . one day **you're going to get old**.

One day **you're going to die** – in a hundred years or so we'll all be dust or ash.

In fact a website, www.deathclock.com, has been set up to tell you when you're going to die and how many seconds you have to live!

Of course, none of that interests you now.

That's why you (speaking in general terms, of course):

(Write the following on a chart and ask for any other life-threatening suggestions.)

- smoke
- drink
- sleep around
- take drugs
- eat too much
- live life in the fast lane

. . . as if there's no tomorrow.

Because all of these, to a different extent, will probably have some effect on . . . when you die.

It's your body, you're free to abuse it as much as you like.

But is there more?

What **does** happen when you die? Is there an afterlife or are the lights just switched off? And if there's an afterlife, are we to be judged? What about heaven and hell?

Just think – one day we're all going to find out – even the existentialist who believes all this is an illusion anyway and may be in for a nasty shock!

Sooner for some. *(Point to list on chart.)*

And, whatever you may think about it now . . . there can only be one truth.

They can't all be right.

Discussion

Canvas people's views on life after death. Is this a subject that people are comfortable discussing or do they think that it's all too morbid? They must all know someone who has had an untimely death – they may want to talk about this, but tact and sensitivity will be needed.

Parting shot

If you died tomorrow, how prepared are you for what comes next?

Useful resources

http://www.77talksforteens.com/talk1.htm

Thinking Clearly about Life after Death by Graham H. Twelftree (Monarch).

2
Who's Pulling Your Strings? Part 1

Theme

A brief look at what influences us, with particular reference to the media in general and television in particular. The objective is to encourage the audience to think for themselves and to be wary of external influences that may not necessarily be in their best interests.

Preparation

Flip chart/OHP. Toy frog (or other small animal), large (transparent) beaker of (cold!) water, quotes to hand out for reading.

Presentation

(Place beaker/flask of water on table.)

Behold a beaker of boiling hot water *(touch it and wince)*.

Behold a frog.

Behold a hot frog *(drop frog into water then toss it sharply upwards)*.

Behold a scalded frog!

Stick a frog into boiling hot water and it jumps a mile. So what?

I now want you to use your imagination. Imagine you were living fifty years ago. It's the 1950s.

Pop music hadn't yet begun. No Nike or Adidas. Celebrities wore hats and nice little moustaches (well, at least the men did). And that box in the corner of your living room – the television – was only starting to appear. Mind you it was an ugly little box with small flickering black and white images and a sound so tinny you'd think it was sponsored by Heinz!

Now take our 1950s person and suddenly transport him fifty years into the future and stick him in front of a 32-inch colour flatscreen widescreen TV with Dolby surround sound.

From watching a grey man in a suit reading the news in the Queen's English he is suddenly faced with a raunchy rap video on MTV, featuring sexy half-dressed girls, gyrating to 130 decibels of music battering his eardrums from five different directions. What's going to happen?

He's going to jump out of his skin – like our frog out of the water – and will probably have a stroke or heart attack! Just like our frog he's just experienced a sudden change and his natural instinct is to escape and protect himself. But unlike our frog he'll probably come back for more!

Culture shock, that's what we call it. Television has changed in fifty years.

Let's examine what he's been used to watching, our 1950s man *(write titles on chart)*:

- "I Love Lucy" – the first sitcom – safe, family values.
- One of the most popular adverts, in the USA, is for "Lucky Strike" cigarettes, with the slogan "Yes, Luckies get our loudest cheers on campus and on dates. With college gals and college guys a Lucky really rates."
- Early science fiction, with wobbly flying saucers, aliens

speaking with New York accents and special effects made out of cardboard and sticky tape.

Some people had high hopes for this medium. *(Give out the following quotes to various people to read out.)*

"Sir Thomas Beecham says he believes that television can do much to improve the musical taste of the nation." *The London Times*, September 1, 1936.

"It is probable that television drama of high calibre and produced by first-rate artists will materially raise the level of dramatic taste of the American nation." David Sarnoff, then President of the Radio Corporation of America, 1939.

Others weren't so sure.

"Television? The word is half Greek and half Latin. No good will come of it." C.P. Scott, editor, *Manchester Guardian*, 1928.

Discussion

Of course no one here can remember the 1950s, though, if the leader has memories of early TV shows, then a short testimony now should spark off a discussion of how TV has changed over the last decade. Concentrate on the three examples given: sitcoms, adverts and science fiction. Discuss how the level of sex, violence and profanities has changed. You could compare *The Office* with *Only Fools and Horses* on attitudes to sex, early *Star Trek* films with *Lord of the Rings* with regard to depictions of violence.

Challenge

Ask parents and grandparents how TV has changed since they were young.

Useful resources

http://www.77talksforteens.com/talk2.htm

3
Who's Pulling Your Strings? Part 2

Theme

As before.

Preparation

As before, plus means of heating water (symbolic, not actual) such as candle, Bunsen burner, microwave, blowtorch (dummy one).

Presentation

(Place beaker/flask of water on table.)

Last week we dropped our frog into boiling water and it leapt out. We suggested that we'd get the same sort of reaction from a 1950s teenager transported to the present and told to watch our TV! Culture shock!

Behold a beaker of luke-warm water. *(Touch it with no reaction.)*

Behold a frog. *(Let the frog shake out of fear, but stroke it and pacify it.)*

Behold a comfortable frog. *(Drop frog into water and leave it there.)*

(Now give the impression of heating the water slowly – I leave this to your imagination.)

Behold boiling water. Behold cooked frog.

(Take frog out and put it on a plate.)

Any French people here?

Q: So what happened?
A: The frog was cooked slowly, so slowly that it **didn't notice it** – until it was too late – and then it didn't notice it at all, because it was dead – and heading for the nearest French restaurant!

What's this got to do with television? Well . . .

In the same way, we've been exposed to a society and a culture that's been growing gradually worse, but it's been **so gradual that mostly we haven't noticed it**. Unlike the frog we haven't been cooked physically, but we've been damaged just the same, in other ways.

Let's return to our three examples:

- Sitcoms: it's now common in English sitcoms to hear the 'F' word spoken for comic effect and many comedy situations are now based around sexual innuendo. What happened to family values?
- Adverts: in the year 2000 the top ten UK advertisers spent almost £500,000,000 on TV advertising. For that outlay, they expect results, so adverts have become more sophisticated and persuasive.
- Science fiction: these days special effects are awesome. Virtually every murky quirk of the film-maker's mind can be digitally reproduced, resulting in images that can be obscene, provocative and highly disturbing.

Some more quotes. *(Give out following quotes to various people to read out.)*

"I must say that I find television very educational. The minute somebody turns it on, I go to the library and read a book." Groucho Marx, American comedian.

"Television is an invention that permits you to be entertained in your living room by people you wouldn't have in your home." David Frost, TV personality.

"Television: chewing gum for the eyes." Frank Lloyd Wright, American architect.

Discussion

How did we get to this position from those sweet, simple days in the 1950s? And does it really matter? What harm do you think there is in what we see on TV these days? *(Guide conversation towards the issue of morality, i.e. how our behaviour is modelled on people we see on the TV in such shows as* EastEnders, Buffy the Vampire Slayer *and* Friends.*)*

Presentation

In the UK, teenagers spend an average of two to three hours a day watching TV. Over 80% of you have TV sets in your bedrooms and virtually all of you, according to a survey, watch TV after the so-called nine o'clock "watershed".

We can understand our frog example better when we look at the difference between the 1950s and now. How did sitcoms lose their family values and gain sexual liberation? How did those clumsy amateur adverts become Guinness with its stampeding horses and insistent soundtrack? How did our cardboard aliens become the Borg? *(You may want to use more up-to-date examples.)*

We didn't see it coming, it just happened. Resistance is futile!

In the 1950s, you could go out and leave your front door unlocked, bikes could be left in front gardens, inner city streets were safe at night, Sunday was still a rest day with all the shops closed, and 20% of you went to church.

Today everything has to be locked up. We need CCTV cameras in our streets to help the police, and Sunday's a day for shopping and DIY, except for the 3% or so of you in church.

So TV has changed in those fifty years and so has society.

If there was no such thing as TV, would society have got so much worse so quickly? What would influence us?

Who's pulling your strings?

Are we, at the end of the day, just muppets? *(Which, these days, is teen-speak for "stupid ineffectual person.")*

Discussion

So who **is** pulling our strings?

Suggested conversation points:

- Where do we get our input for morality and behaviour?
- Who influences us most? Family, friends, teachers – how are these people influenced?
- What about influence from the church? Remind them that the bedrock of Western society is the moral structure as taught by the Christian church.
- How are we affected by issues such as abortion, teenage pregnancies, violence, euthanasia and homosexuality that are increasingly being covered on TV programmes, including those aimed at children?
- What are the driving forces of the people who create TV

programmes? If money is the main motive, rather than our moral or spiritual well-being, isn't this a worry?

Parting shot

How much are your attitudes shaped by what you see on TV? Let's say you saw a documentary on how ordinary Germans played a direct role in the wickedness of the Nazi Germany. How would that affect your view of any German you might meet tomorrow?

Useful resources

http://www.77talksforteens.com/talk3.htm

4
Dreaming of Little Green Men

Theme

An examination of the science fiction theme of aliens and asking whether a possible reason for their popularity is our need for an "external power" to help sort out humanity's problems.

Preparation

Flip chart/OHP, copy of poster for *E.T.* film (see website).

Presentation

How many science fiction films can you list involving aliens visiting earth? Which of these have the aliens as the "good guys" and which have them as the "bad guys"?

(Write names on chart in either of two columns, "good guys" and "bad guys". Examples of the first are: E.T. *and* Close Encounters of the Third Kind. *Examples of the second are:* Independence Day, War of the Worlds *and* Mars Attacks.*)*

Discussion

First let's look at the "bad guys" films. There's a lot of them. Why do you think they are so popular? *(Write suggestions on chart. Most probable reason is popularity of good versus evil films, regardless of genre, such as war films and "cowboys and indians".)*

Presentation

(Display poster of E.T. *film.)* But what of the others? Why is
E.T. the third most popular film of all time, earning more than
$700 million worldwide? Let's have a closer look.

A famous writer, Martin Amis, known for his cynicism and
worldliness, had this to say about the film:

"Towards the end of *E.T.*, barely able to support my own grief
and bewilderment, I turned and looked down the aisle at my
fellow sufferers; executive, black dude, Japanese businessman,
punk, hippie, mother, teenager, child. Each face was a mask of
tears . . . And we weren't crying for the little extraterrestrial,
nor for little Elliott, nor for little Gertie. We were crying for our
lost selves."

Discussion

Does anyone share these feelings? Share thoughts and emotions
provoked by this film.

Presentation

Let's dip into the story.

- When E.T. first appears, he's hunted by scientists, who want
  to capture him and probably harm him. *(Write "hunted
  down" on chart.)*
- E.T. is hidden from these scientists by three children. *(Write
  "hidden" on chart.)*
- Although E.T. is wise, with supernatural powers, he
  explores his surroundings with the innocence and curiosity
  of a child. *(Write "wise but innocent" on chart.)*
- E.T. heals his best friend, Elliott, by touching him with his
  finger. *(Write "healer" on chart.)*

- E.T. is finally captured by the scientists and dies. As he lies in his coffin, Elliott says, "I'll believe in you all of my life". *(Write "dies" on chart.)*
- E.T. returns to life. Elliott rushes to his brother, screaming, "He's alive! He's alive!" *(Write "returns to life" on chart.)*
- E.T. along with the two brothers, escapes and appears to the other boys who had helped him earlier. *(Write "appears to friends" on chart.)*
- The spaceship lands and E.T. leaves Earth but, before that, he says goodbye to Elliott by touching the boy's forehead and saying "I'll be right here". *(Write "says goodbye" on chart.)*

The writer of *E.T.*, Steven Spielberg, is a Jew with no interest in Christianity but, to Christians, the theme of the film is familiar, very familiar indeed. *(You may wish to expand on this and explore further.)*

Why do you think there is such an interest in UFOs these days? Are we looking for aliens who are going to wipe us out, as in *War of the Worlds* or *Independence Day*, or aliens who are going to put us right and show us the way?

Parting shot

E.T., along with many "friendly alien" films, succeeds because it touches something inside us, a need we all have for something outside of ourselves to help us. Perhaps E.T. has already come?

Useful resources

http://www.77talksforteens.com/talk4.htm

5
Godfrey and Edward Discuss the Big Bang

Theme

Some scientists over the past few decades have been attempting to describe the origins of the universe with the aim of squeezing out the idea of a Creator God and replacing Him with scientific theories. Lately their research has led them to a disturbing and (for them) unwelcome conclusion and their story provides a better scientific apologetic for the existence of God than many Christians could ever have come up with!

Preparation

This has been prepared as a dialogue between two scientists, Godfrey Andhappy (the atheist) and Edward P. Raysalot (the Christian). They will sit face to face. The leader should play one role, the other should be played by a competent volunteer. You will need to photocopy the relevant pages, or the whole dialogue can be downloaded from the website. For added dramatic and comic effect, if you have any talented actors, have two of them miming the parts of God and science in the background, responding to the material as it is read out.

Presentation

GODFREY: Look, as far as I see it, mankind is not at the centre of the universe. We are not important, we're an accident, a random event.

EDWARD: And where is your proof? We're scientists, aren't we? You can't just say these things without proof.

GODFREY: Yes, and where is your proof for God? Eh?

EDWARD: Some things are unprovable scientifically speaking. This is where faith comes into it. Anyway, if God didn't create the universe, who did?

GODFREY: The big bang, of course.

EDWARD: Which is?

GODFREY: A quantum singularity.

EDWARD: Which is?

GODFREY: An expanding bubble of quantum foam appearing from nothingness.

EDWARD: Which is?

GODFREY: Lots of very hot matter expanding very fast from one point.

EDWARD: That's better. Now those thickies can understand better. Now tell me this. Who produced the big bang? Who lit the blue touch paper?

GODFREY: I suppose you want me to say . . . God. Well, I won't, because we don't need him. We've explained him away by the Heisenberg Uncertainty Principle.

EDWARD: Which is?

GODFREY: You see, Edward, when we first discovered . . . and proved . . . that it was the big bang that created the universe back in the 1950s and 1960s, we had that very problem to consider of "why did it happen". At that time you Christians had a good time mocking us so, to our shame, we just swept the whole thing under the carpet. That was until the 1970s when we figured it out.

EDWARD: The Heisenberg . . . Uncertainty . . . Principle?

GODFREY: Yes.

EDWARD: Which is?

GODFREY: Heisenberg proved that if x is the position co-ordinate of an electron in a specific state, and p is the momentum of that electron, and that each have been independently measured for many electrons in the specific state, then: delta times delta p is greater or equal to h/2 where delta x is the precision of x, and delta p is the precision of the momentum co-ordinates, and h is Plank's constant.

EDWARD: *(pauses)* Yes, I see *(pauses, then gesticulates to the audience, encouraging them to say, "Which is?")*

GODFREY: Basically, you can never know both the position and the speed of any given particle.

EDWARD: And how does this do away with God, this momentous discovery?

GODFREY: *(gestures at audience)* You expect this lot to understand?

EDWARD: No. Just between the two of us. We'll explain it to them afterwards.

GODFREY: Well, the big bang can now be totally explained by physics and quantum mechanics, through the Uncertainty Principle. You see, Heisenberg showed us that, even in the nothingness that came before the big bang, there was this dynamic situation of particles and anti-particles appearing and disappearing out of the "Quantum foam", always cancelling each other out. It's wonderful, it's elegant . . .

EDWARD: And when did this "quantum foam" decide to bang? *(He gestures)*.

GODFREY: That's irrelevant. We're talking about a situation outside of time, space, matter and energy.

EDWARD: And this does away with God?

GODFREY: Of course, it's marvellous!

EDWARD: OK. Then what about the universe itself, this universe created by this random big bang? Why was gravity just right? Also electromagnetism, the size of electrons and protons. You know as well as I do that if just one of these factors was just an eensy bit different, life as we know it would just not have happened.

GODFREY: Yes, yes. We're working on that problem. We're

waiting for the "Theory of Everything". That will explain it all.

EDWARD: And when's that going to arrive?

GODFREY: We're patient. One day

EDWARD: And in the meantime?

GODFREY: Yes, there's this other exciting theory, in fact it's the latest "big idea" among us physicists. All we have to do is consider that our universe is just one out of trillions of possible ones.

EDWARD: Oh, I see. Our universe is the only one where the natural laws of gravity, etc., are just right for life to exist and for you and me to be able to sit here discussing these things.

GODFREY: Yes!

EDWARD: So our universe exists in order for humans to exist, as we wouldn't exist in any of the other ones?

GODFREY: Yes.

EDWARD: So our universe has been created for . . . humans?

GODFREY: Mmmmm.

EDWARD: So physicists are willing to accept that humans are the centre of the universe? And there's only one possible explanation for this to be so, for the natural laws to be just right, for atoms to be just the right size, etc. There's only one possible reason.

GODFREY: *(pauses)* Which is?

EDWARD: GOD!

Discussion

The conversation between the scientists represents current scientific thinking on the subject of God and creation. If there is time and the group are motivated then talk about all the things that had to be "just right" for life to exist, then ask if it is reasonable for this all to be a "random" event.

Parting shot

If God is as all-powerful as Christians claim, surely he is able to create our universe out of nothing, just like that!

Useful resources

http://www.77talksforteens.com/talk5.htm

God, Time and Stephen Hawking by David Wilkinson (Monarch).
Thinking Clearly about God and Science by Rob Frost and David Wilkinson (Monarch).

6
Posh 'n' Becks Ate My Parrot

Theme

The nature of celebrity: human beings have an inbuilt need to worship. In teenagers this is often expressed in the veneration of "celebrities", usually taken from the fields of sport, film or music. It is a useful exercise to analyse this need and, while not denying it, point them in other more useful and worthwhile directions.

Preparation

Flip chart/OHP to illustrate key points. Large mirror and red lipstick.

Presentation

(Write title at top. Title should provoke a giggle and lighten the atmosphere.)

Posh 'n' Becks? What's that, a new life form? It might as well be for all the attention we give it. It's probably the best example, particularly in the UK, of a "celebrity". In this case we are looking at a very special case, a combination of sport and the worlds of music and fashion.

Once upon a time there were two human beings, living a few miles apart near London. One could balance a ball on his head better than most and the other pouted a lot. One was pretty, with charisma and a high chirpy voice – and the other joined the Spice Girls! Both were "celebrities" in their own right, but became "super-celebrities" the day they became "an item".

(Write the word "celebrity".)

So, what is a celebrity?

The Oxford Dictionary says: it's "the condition of being much talked about".

So why are we so interested in talking, reading and dreaming about Victoria "Posh" Adams and David "Becks" Beckham? Is it because she's a good singer and he's a great footballer?

(Ask for a show of hands as to which of the two is the more talented.)

Is it because they are both rich and attractive? Yes, of course it is! Is it because they are everything we're not? Perhaps. Thinking about it, then, if we're going to spend our time talking, reading and dreaming about a "celebrity", we might as well stick with this pair, as they do it better than most.

My next question is, why? Why are they talked about? This is not a superficial, easy, "Why", this is a deeper, more personal "Why?"

(Write a large "?" after the word "Celebrity".)

Are we so fed up of our own lives that we need to live our lives through other people? Do we care more about the exploits of "Posh 'n' Becks" than the family across the street? Is a TV soap more real to you than your own family life?

Who matters more to you – your neighbours or those Aussie "Neighbours"? If you're honest, it's probably the life of the celebrity, or the soap family that has more meaning for you.

Discussion

If you were alone on a desert island and were allowed one companion, who would it be and why? A friend, a member of your family, or a celebrity?

Presentation

You've got to face the facts, you'll never be a "Posh" or a "Becks". In fact, to be honest, you should never want to be a "Posh" or a "Becks".

Q: What is the downside to celebrity?
A: Lack of privacy, danger of stalkers, too much money.

I'm not joking about that last one. They say that, before marrying the girl, look at the mother, because that's what she'll be like in 20 years or so! In the same way, the news is full of aged celebrities, lives wrecked by . . . too much money. With the money came drugs, drink, overindulgence, divorce and loneliness. Look at them – they were the "Posh 'n' Becks" of their day, but look at them now. They don't all go that way but, all too often, that's the price they pay for overdoing it when they had the looks, the talent, the money.

But that's their lives. **It's your life that's more important** . . . well, for you, anyway. So, how's the best way to live your own life? The most important thing is to be real, be yourself. Don't try to be what you're not.

(Point mirror at the audience.)

You are who you are created to be, nothing more and nothing less. You are unique, there's only one of you. Is that good?

Discussion

Ask for a show of hands to see who are happy that there's only one like them. For those who seem to think little of themselves, be affirming with words like "you should think more highly of yourself". For those who think too much of themselves, think of a suitable put-down like "OK, big head, one of you is probably enough for this world!"

Presentation

Every individual life is precious, every life has meaning. *(Write on chart.)*

Sometimes it's hard for us to understand, when we see babies dying in a famine, or megalomaniac dictators treating lives cheaply. But that doesn't make it any less true.

So make your life count. The point is that you've got a whole life ahead of you. Not just today and tomorrow but maybe another seventy years or so.

The choices you make now will probably determine who and what you'll be for years to come. So make the right choices. Find your own path, don't waste your life immersed in the fantasies thrown at you by TV, films and magazines.

(Write the words "be real" on the mirror with red lipstick.)

Be real. Speak to real people. Get into your own family. Ask your grandad what he did in the war (if you've got a whole evening to spend). Ask your dad what he was doing when President Kennedy or John Lennon was shot.

(Underline the words "be real".)

Be real. The most important thing you can do is live your life as your own. It's the only one you're going to get this side of death. Don't waste it on the trivial. Does it really matter what Becks has for breakfast, or who Robbie went swimming with? If it does, then at least file the information away in the part of your brain labelled "useless information", and now **get on with your own life.**

And what's that about Posh 'n' Becks eating my parrot? It was just to grab your attention, and who cares anyway?

Have a wonderful life!

Parting shot

"You were born an original. Don't die a copy." John Mason, American author.

Useful resources

http://www.77talksforteens.com/talk6.htm

7
The Snowflake and the Flower

Theme

An examination of beauty found in nature and what it implies.
This approach is different in that God is never mentioned and
the hope is that any debate that ensues will naturally bring up
the subject of God, from the group itself.

Preparation

OHP/flip chart to illustrate points. A flower (with petals) or a
picture of one. A picture showing an example of architectural
beauty, e.g. a Roman column. A picture of a snowflake.

Presentation

(Show picture of Roman column, or similar.)

Q: Look at this beautiful Roman column. What was it used for?
A: Holding up part of a building.

(Draw on the chart a simple unadorned column.)

Q: Then why didn't they just use a long slab of concrete?
Wouldn't it have done the same job at a fraction of the
cost?
A: It isn't as nice to look at. It has no beauty.

We sometimes add beautiful features to things we make for no
other reason than to be pleasant on the eye.

Now consider this:

47

- Why don't birds make a grating sound when they sing to each other?
- Why doesn't the English Lakeland look ugly, as it's only a geological oddity?
- Why doesn't a sunset make you feel nauseated?
- Why don't snowflakes have random patterns when you look at them closely?

These might seem strange ideas but, think about it, there's no practical, useful reason why these things should be beautiful . . . yet they are.

- Birds **do** make a pleasant sound when they sing to each other.
- The English Lakeland **does** look beautiful and attract thousands of visitors every year.
- And a sunset **can** be incredible.
- Snowflakes **do** have perfect symmetrical shapes, but each one is different.

Let's look closer at one. *(Show picture of a snowflake.)*

- It's virtually impossible to find two that are identical.
- They are all perfectly symmetrical from all directions.
- They have beauty, even though there's no real reason for it.

Consider this flower. *(Show it.)*

Think of the colour – it's colourful ironically because it's starved of water (the leaves get most of the sap) yet the end-product is pleasing to the eye (as well as to the bee and the butterfly).

Think of the patterns – the closer you look the more intricate they are, too small even for the eyes of a bee or butterfly. Under a microscope you begin to see their beauty.

Think of their smell – to attract bees, but why do we need to find it pleasant?

Discussion

What's the point of beauty? Is beauty in nature an accident and, if so, how come it's such an "enjoyable" accident? Would these things be beautiful if we weren't around to observe them?

Parting shot

If the beauty of the flower and snowflake has no practical use, would it have evolved or could someone have put it there?

Useful resources

http://www.77talksforteens.com/talk7.htm

Hallmarks of Design, by Stuart Burgess (Day One).

8
What is Life?

Theme

A look at the facts and realities of abortion and what this tells us about how we value life.

Preparation

OHP/flipchart. Picture of swan. Bearing in mind the subject of this talk, it would be good to be prepared if any girls in the group have already had an upsetting experience. Literature can be obtained from organisations listed on the website.

Presentation

(Show picture.)

Imagine a swan, elegant and regal in its bearing, gliding over the water. What we don't see is that, below the waterline, it is frantically paddling away like a drowning rat!

This image is usually used to illustrate that when something appears to be running smoothly, it is usually because of frantic efforts behind the scenes (e.g. TV programmes, award ceremonies).

But we can also use it to illustrate the situation of **out of sight out of mind** – just because you can't see it, it doesn't mean that it ain't there or has no value!

This brings us to the topic for today: **abortions** – terminations.

This talk is not to make judgements or offer advice. It is just to make you think about something very important.

How we value life. *(Write on chart.)*

When does life start? At conception, at birth or at some time in between? (If so, when?) *(Ask for a show of hands.)*

Birth is not the start of a new human life, just a change of the baby's environment. *(Write on chart.)*

So let's look at the timescale.

It all begins in the womb when a single sperm cell from the father fertilises an egg from the mother.

At that moment all the features of the new human being are established, including colour of eyes, gender and build. All the information about how the baby is to grow and develop is contained in those original two cells.

Has life started? *(Every time you say this tell the group to raise their hands if they agree and keep them raised.)*

At five weeks, the heart starts beating. **Has life started?**

At six weeks, the baby has a complete skeleton. **Has life started?**

At nine weeks, the baby has fingerprints. **Has life started?**

At ten weeks, the baby can swallow. **Has life started?**

At eleven weeks, the baby is sensitive to touch. **Has life started?**

At twelve weeks, the baby is aware of sound and can sneeze. **Has life started?**

Most abortions are done between the eighth and twelfth week –
so what does that mean for those of you with your hands up?

Discussion

So, is abortion murder, or is the foetus not yet what we would
call a "person"?

Presentation

In Britain there are 160,000 to 180,000 abortions a year –
nearly 500 a day – one every three minutes.

Since abortions have been made legal, there have been **over 5
million abortions** in Britain.

Although more than 90% of abortions are certified as being
done to safeguard the mother's physical or mental health, it is
widely recognised that most of these abortions are performed
for convenience.

These are hard facts and very upsetting, more so for some than
for others.

The real problem is our society – we can't help living in a
society that makes it possible for things like abortion to take
place.

When I told you the fact that there have been over 5 million
abortions in Britain, what would you have thought if I had said
that over 5 million babies have been **legally killed** in Britain?

Aren't I saying the same thing?

(Point to chart.) Birth is not the start of a new human life –
just a change of the baby's environment.

(Note: some people may be upset, or may even need counselling, as a result of this material. Please use the references on the web page for further help.)

Parting shot

We all carry with us the possibilities for new life. Treasure it for the precious gift that it is.

Useful resources

http://www.77talksforteens.com/talk8.htm

9
Natural Born Killers?

Theme

Using a historical illustration, we examine the darker side of human motivation by considering the question, "in which situations is it right to kill?"

Preparation

OHP/flip chart. Write war slogan on it: "Your country, right or wrong."

Presentation

(Ask for suggestions for other war slogans e.g. "The only good . . . is a dead . . .".)

Consider this situation. It is a time of war. You are in a group of 500, who have been ordered to assemble in a village square by a Major. He tells you that you all have an important mission. This mission will result in the deaths of many of the enemy. He also gives you a choice. You can either accept the mission or not, and if you decline the mission there will be no consequences – no firing squad or court martial.

Discussion

What would you do? Consider the relevant factors:

- It is a war and it's a case of kill or be killed.
- The wider picture – what will happen to your family or nation if the war is lost?

- Is the cause **a just** cause?
- Is it your duty to follow orders in a time of war, and is it cowardice not to?

Presentation

Now let's fill in a few more facts of our war story.

You are not, in fact, a soldier by profession. You are middle aged, a metal worker with a small family. You agree to the mission. You are led into a forest, where a long line of innocent civilians – men, women and children – are waiting for you. You are to be part of the firing squad.

Discussion

What has changed? It is still a war situation and bombs are being dropped on civilian populations on both sides. They are still the enemy, but not soldiers. Is there a difference? Would you still shoot?

Presentation

In 1942, at the height of the Second World War, a German reserve police battalion from Hamburg were given the mission of rounding up and massacring over 38,000 Jews in a village in Poland. The average age of these Germans was 39, they were middle class and most had no particular hatred of Jews. About a dozen out of the 500 refused to take part, and some more refused to carry on once the shooting had started, but the majority got on with it. Later on, some actually developed a taste for the job and actively volunteered to take part in other death squads. They had acquired a taste for killing and it didn't concern them.

One of them said this: "It was possible for me to shoot just the children. It so happened that the mothers led the children by the hand. My neighbour shot the mother and I shot the child, because I reasoned that the child couldn't live without its mother. This soothed my conscience."

They were just following orders. As one man later admitted, it was not until years later that he began to consider that what he had done had not been right. He had not given it a thought at the time.

Discussion

Was this just a one-off, a Nazi German thing? Could you see yourself in their position, given all the circumstances?

Presentation

An important point is that this was not a one-off. It still happens. *(You can mention Rwanda as a modern-day example, perhaps.)*

Even Americans have been guilty. You may have heard of the My Lai massacre in the Vietnam war in 1968, when American soldiers massacred 500 unarmed women, children and old men in a four-hour shooting spree.

Has anyone seen the film *Natural Born Killers*?

The theme of the film is that all humans are murderers, or have the potential to be. Some admit it and act it out, others deny it. The police, the prison officials, the FBI agent and even the journalist in the movie are all murderers when the moment presents itself.

So have we learned anything about ourselves?

The atrocities in Nazi Germany, in Vietnam and elsewhere were not necessarily committed by evil people, just ordinary people like you and me, in extraordinary circumstances. But all these people showed that they were **capable of evil**. Are we any different?

Parting shot

Do you think we are all capable of acts of evil or is this something unique to just a few?

Useful resources

http://www.77talksforteens.com/talk9.htm

Ordinary Men by Christopher Browning (Harper Perennial).

10
The Watchmaker's Guide to the Universe. Part 1

Theme

Looking at an example of design and encouraging the audience to consider the possibility that where there is design there must also be a designer. An apologetic for the existence of God (without getting too heavily into Paley's full arguments).

Preparation

Old (preferably broken) analogue watch, mallet. Sign made of card, with "1" printed on it.

Presentation

Who's got the time? My watch has stopped. *(Get audience response.)*

(Try to adjust your watch, pull it off in exasperation, put it on a table and smash it to smithereens with the mallet. Collect all the parts into your hand and offer it to the audience.)

Can anyone put my watch together again so that it works?

No? Can anyone here lend me a watch? *(Still hold the mallet menacingly.)*

(Take watch from audience – with assurances that it will come to no harm. Ask where it came from, making the point that the watch didn't just appear ready made but was bought from a shop, who in turn bought it from a manufacturer, who made the thing.)

So someone made the watch, it didn't just appear on your arm one day. *(Give watch back.)*

In schools and in society in general we are taught that all living things – animals, fish, birds and human beings, evolved over millions of years from a lump of mush. As far as society and schools are concerned it's the truth, no argument.

It's called the **Theory of Evolution** and, like all theories, it's just a theory, there to be shot at.

Some Christians, believing in a God who created life and the universe, have problems with Charles Darwin's theory of evolution, and today we are going to look at one piece of evidence against this theory.

Over 200 years ago a clergyman called William Paley said that, just as a watch is too complicated to have just sprung into existence at random, so all living things, ourselves included – far more complicated than a watch – must also have been created **by a creator**.

We don't show off our Rolex to our friends and say, "Yes, all I did was collect all the cogs and springs and wheels together and waited a few hundred thousand years and they . . . just evolved into this lovely watch."

So . . . evidence number one for the defence . . . my watch.

(Place bits of watch on table, against a sign with number 1 on it.)

Discussion

Evolution is taught in school as fact, yet Christians believe in a God who created the universe. Is it possible to believe in both?

Could God create the world **through** the complex process of evolution?

Parting shot

We readily believe that a watch has a designer, why shouldn't we think the same for the human body, which is a million times more complex? "In the absence of any other proof, the thumb alone would convince me of God's existence." Isaac Newton.

Useful resources

http://www.77talksforteens.com/talk10.htm

11
The Watchmaker's Guide
to the Universe. Part 2

Theme

As in Part 1.

Preparation

Smashed up watch. Two signs made of card, with "1" and "2" printed on them. Picture of night sky, galaxies.

Presentation

Last week we presented this broken watch as our first evidence for the existence of a designer. Someone has to put this watch together again. It can't evolve back into a watch!

Next we're going from one extreme to another. From our humble watch, to the universe. If we're going to see a creator in action, then the universe is a good place to start.

Now a few years ago scientists made an amazing discovery called the **Anthropic Principle**. It's a bit tricky to explain, so I'll ease you into it gradually.

Q: Anyone here who owns a computer?
Q: Keep hands up – all those who've ever needed to have things fixed on the computer?

Computers are complex bits of machinery. For one to work, a whole group of other things have to be working properly.

Q: Name the components of a computer.

A: CPU, monitor, disk drive, CD-ROM drive, hard disk, keyboard, mouse, modem, video card, audio card, I/O card, speakers, power supply, operating system, software, etc.

If one of these things goes wrong, the computer will work below par, if at all.

The computer has been designed so that every component works efficiently in combination with every other component, with the end result of providing a tool for us to use – usually for playing games (what a waste of technology!).

Now back to the universe. I told you about this amazing discovery made by these scientists, the Anthropic Principle. What they discovered is this:

The universe appears as if it were specifically designed for the existence and well-being of human beings.

It might sound obvious, but only to those of us who believe in God, the creator. These were scientists, who were mostly not Christian and more than likely believers in the theory of evolution.

Yet here they were saying that this universe, supposedly produced at random by some big bang event billions of years ago, containing billions of stars, billions of miles apart, only existed for the inhabitants of the third planet of a minor star in some backwater of the Milky Way. Awesome!

They were "this close" to admitting the existence of a "Supreme Being", a God, who created it all . . . for us.

But why should they be saying this? **What's the evidence?**

There's a load of it but it can be summarised in two statements:

- Even very slight changes in the laws of nature would have made it impossible for life to exist.
- Human life would not have been possible if it weren't for a large number of very improbable things happening.

Here's a partial list. Remember, if there was even the slightest change in any of these, life simply wouldn't exist.

- The rate of spin of the earth.
- The length of a year.
- The tilt of the earth.
- The distance of the earth from the sun.
- The type of orbit of the earth.
- The diameter of the earth.
- The thickness of the earth's crust.
- The colour of the sun.
- The size of the sun.
- The proportion of oxygen in the air.
- The right level of gravitation.

So if any of these things had changed even very slightly, life on earth wouldn't have existed. If this doesn't speak of a creator, rather than blind evolution, then nothing does!

Sir Fred Hoyle, world renowned astronomer, stated: "Commonsense interpretation of the facts is that a super-intelligence has monkeyed with physics, as well as chemistry and biology, and that there are no blind forces in nature." And he didn't believe in God at that time!

This is a fascinating subject and, for those of you who want to do some research, I'll give you a web address to find out more from. *(Or you can print it off yourself and give out the article.)*

So . . . piece of evidence number two for the defence . . . the universe.

(Place picture of universe on table, against a sign with number 2 on it.)

Discussion

Ask if any of the group are doing science subjects and if so, try and get them to explain some of the terms used. Play devil's advocate and try to defend the idea of chance and natural selection when confronted with the facts presented in this talk. How can "chance" have had anything to do with such things as the size of the earth, distance from the sun, etc?

Parting shot

If the universe has come about by chance, how can chance produce such ideal situations for life to thrive on earth?

Useful resources

http://www.77talksforteens.com/talk11.htm

He Made the Stars Also by Stuart Burgess (Day One).

TANGY ORANGE SECTION

Asking Questions

12
Did You Hear the One About . . . ?

Theme

Looking at urban legends and how they are spread. Compare them with a "legend" that swept through Jerusalem about a rabbi who was crucified a few days before but who had since been seen alive!

Preparation

OHP/flip chart.

Presentation

Listen to the following statements.

"Did you know why 'Kentucky Fried Chicken' changed their name to KFC? It's because they can't use the word 'chicken' in the title, ever since it was found out that they don't use chickens any more. Instead they cook genetically manipulated organisms, kept alive by tubes inserted into their bodies to pump blood and nutrients throughout their structure. They have no beaks, no feathers, and no feet. Their bone structure is dramatically shrunk to get more meat out of them."

"Did you know that if you tip a Coca Cola can on its side and read the script logo, it shows a figure snorting a line of cocaine, as a reference to the fact that cocaine is a key ingredient of the drink?"

"And as for Pepsi, did you know that when they launched in China, their slogan, 'come alive with Pepsi', when translated into Chinese, became 'Pepsi brings your ancestors back from the dead'?"

Actually, two of these statements are lies, "urban legends" we call them. These are stories that zip around the world – usually by e-mail these days – to entertain us and confuse us, depending on how gullible we are.

Q: Which one is true?
A: The Pepsi Cola one – though it didn't seem to stop it selling like hot cakes!

Here's another one:

"Did you hear about the guru from the East who was killed by the authorities, then buried in a guarded tomb? Apparently the guards fell asleep and friends of the guru stole his body so they could pretend he came back to life."

This one is 2000 years old and was the official explanation for the "strange case of the disappearing body of Jesus", which Christians call "the resurrection".

Q: Using the examples given, what is often the purpose of an urban legend?
A: To defame or discredit or cause doubt.

The resurrection is the single most important historic fact of the Christian faith. Paul, one of the main writers of the New Testament, admitted that if the resurrection was ever shown to be false then Christianity would collapse like a house of cards.

So what better way for its opponents to discredit it than to create an **urban legend**?

Trouble is, this one was full of holes!

Read the Jesus "legend" again.

(Draw a series of large holes on the chart and write each point – in summary form – inside each hole.)

- Roman guards worked in groups of 16 – at any time **at least four** would have been fully awake – so to say guards were asleep was ridiculous.
- The tomb was **sealed** by a massive two-ton stone, put into place by the soldiers. This would have had to be removed – in silence.
- This urban legend was backed up by a point of a **sword** for any who cared to doubt the official words of the Roman authorities.

And after his resurrection Jesus was seen, so the Bible says, by his group of followers, at least twelve times over a 40-day period.

Discussion

Air any feedback or objections. If there aren't any because the listeners are too sceptical about Christianity even to care, then carry on with the following statement.

Presentation

For those of you who say: "That's all very well for you to quote from the Bible, but I don't believe in it. These are just stories, these people you mention may not have even existed – prove it!"

Consider this.

- Whether you believe it or not, Christianity is with us now and it had to come from somewhere.
- There had to be some historical facts that formed the basis for this new religion, 2000 years ago – even if you don't believe in the Bible account.
- Non-Christian Roman historians tell us that the Christians were very well known – who else were fed to the lions, butchered by gladiators and abused by such emperors as Caligula and Nero?
- Something significant must have happened for these Christians to live the lives they did and die the deaths they did.
- Tracking backwards, these Christians must have been taught their faith by other Christians, who themselves would have been taught. This must have gone right back to the "First Christians".
- These "First Christians" must have been those present at the death of Jesus. Despite the "urban legend", they must have encountered something very real and important, significant and life-changing enough for them to be willing to die for their faith.
- All of Jesus' main followers (apart from one, who was exiled), met with gory deaths.
- There must be **something** in it.

Discussion

Would you be prepared to die for something that you weren't fully convinced was true and worth dying for? Soldiers in a war situation are a different case, as they are acting to protect their families and nation. Christians have died (and still are dying) to "protect" their faith – surely that is significant?

Parting shot

How do you personally reach the point in deciding whether something is true or not?

Useful resources

http://www.77talksforteens.com/talk12.htm

13
Think First

Theme

A look at the "Golden Rule" as a guideline for behaviour.

Preparation

OHP/flipchart. A wooden ruler sprayed with gold paint.

Presentation

You are Arnold Schwarzenegger. Armed with the latest in firearm technology you go in search of the evil man who killed your best friend in the jungles of Borneo. You find him in the act of torturing your other best friend with a meathook. You see red and decide to act. What do you do?

1. Waste him without hesitation?
2. Reason with him then waste him?
3. Reason with him then take him captive?
4. Forgive him and let him off?

(Have a show of hands.)

The chances are that you choose option one. After all, it's expected for an action hero.

You are *(insert name of someone in the group)*. Someone has "borrowed" your walkman. Armed with the latest in put downs, withering stares and juicy expletives, you set off and corner the suspect in the act of using the disputed object. What do you do?

1. Let rip with your tongue?
2. Grab the walkman then let rip with your tongue?
3. Reason with them, then grab the walkman?
4. Be nice to them and come to an agreement?

(Have a show of hands.)

Not so straightforward. You act, but this is the real world. **You have to think first.**

Discussion

And how do you do this? Are you worried about consequences of your actions, in terms of broken friendships or other people's feelings, or does this not bother you? If it doesn't, why not? Otherwise, what rules do you use?

Presentation

(Show the ruler.)

This is the best rule to use: **the Golden Rule**.

Q: What is the Golden Rule?
A: Treat others as you want to be treated.
Q: And where did this Golden Rule come from?
A: Religion.

The Golden Rule didn't just appear as a good idea by some bright spark. It is found in the scriptures of every major religion. In Christianity it is in the Gospel of Matthew:

(Write on chart.) Do for others what you want them to do for you.

Easy to see – but easy to do?

Arnold Schwarzenegger (in his movies anyway) lives by the Golden Rule. He shoots first and talks later (with words of one syllable) – but would expect others to do the same to him (if they were quick and brave enough!).

How about you? Returning to our walkman borrower, it is worth thinking things through before acting. It may be that there was a breakdown in communication and the other person has borrowed your walkman in good faith. Would you want to be falsely accused of stealing?

Do for others what you want them to do for you.

For some, Christianity is just a set of rules and regulations. For a Christian it just boils down to one, the Golden Rule. *(You can quote them Mark 12:28–31 if they are interested.)*

Discussion

Does this sound like a good rule? Any examples or testimonies of this in action?

Parting Shot

If everyone followed the Golden Rule, whether individuals or nations, what a great world we'd be living in!

Useful resources

http://www.77talksforteens.com/talk13.htm

14
A Journey Backwards
Into Truth. Part 1

Theme

Introducing the idea of the Bible not just as a religious book, but as a book of history, featuring real stories in the real world.

Preparation

Find posters or magazine pictures of Princess Diana, John Lennon and President Kennedy or any contemporary figure who has figured recently in the news. Display them prominently. Connect them all with string, attached by paperclips, the rest of the string still in a roll, held in your hand. Also have ready other pictures (depicting Second World War, First World War, Battle of Hastings, Jesus on the cross, Old Testament theme) and a big Bible.

Presentation

Do you remember where you were the day that the World Trade Center was destroyed or Princess Diana died (or any other recent major international event)? You probably do. Ask older people the same question about John Lennon's murder, or about President Kennedy's assassination. The chances are that they have some memory of these events. These are all **historic** events, but all within the lifetimes of people still living. *(Throw the string into the audience – preferably at someone who can catch.)*

We can go back further and there will be people with recollections of the Second World War – usually concentrating on their own heroic deeds.

(Using a paperclip, attach Second World War picture further along the string.)

. . . and even a handful who can go back further to the First World War.

(Attach First World War picture further along the string.)

But we can safely say that, if we go back as far as the nineteenth century, we are looking at a **very small group indeed** – people well over a hundred who will be relying purely on childhood memories, which may not be too reliable.

Going back further, we start having to rely on history books. Yet, although we have no way of checking the facts, we tend to believe what we read, because there is no reason not to. It is taught to us at school and we **know** that teachers never lie.

So let's carry on with our backward journey through time. We arrive at key dates and events that are fixed into the historical story of our nation.

(Attach Battle of Hastings picture a lot further down the string.)

Q: 1066? What does this date signify?
A: Battle of Hastings and the first French tourists in England. In the USA, it could be 1492 with Christopher Columbus, partly responsible for, among other things, importing a selection of weird and wonderful European diseases to the American continent.

But this is not a history lesson; you have enough of this sort of stuff at school or college.

Let's go back further. *(Unravel the string more.)*

What do we do about people like Robin Hood, or King Arthur of Camelot? Are we talking about real people, or legends? At the same time we can go back into what is known as ancient history to tales of Hercules, the gods of Olympus, Jason and the Argonauts.

Are these true stories?

Then there are the Bible stories, which bring us to the Bible itself. Truth or fiction? History or fables?

(Open a large Bible and put it on a table and leave the ball of string on top of it.)

Are we talking about the most important book in the history of the world, according to Christians, or the greatest con in the history of the world, according to its sternest critics?

It's a holy book, in various degrees, to three major religions, umpteen cults and many fringe faiths. It has been read by more people and published in more languages than any other book.

It has been said that if every Bible was destroyed, it could be largely restored by collecting all the Bible quotations from other books available, its influence is so great.

It may not be the trendiest of reading material, or even the easiest to read, but we can't ignore it.

But is it true? Is it historically true?

Discussion

Conduct a straw poll, asking for a show of hands for three opinions on the Bible:

- Totally true.
- Mostly true – except where historians or scientists have "disproved" it.
- Mostly false.

Ask how many in the group come from Christian families and whether their decision is affected by this fact. What is the opinion of their families or schools on this matter? What about the media – how is the Bible and its contents treated in the film world? Do we still get religious epics or do modern films on religious topics have a "lower view" of biblical material?

Parting shot

Like it or not, the Bible has been the most influential book in history, by far. Have you ever opened it to find out why?

Useful resources

http://www.77talksforteens.com/talk14.htm

15
A Journey Backwards
Into Truth. Part 2

Theme

As in Part 1.

Preparation

As before.

Presentation

We've been going backwards into time. From what we see as
recent history, right back to what we call ancient history and
then, to Bible times. We learned that the Bible has been so
influential that **if every Bible was destroyed, it could be largely
restored by collecting all the Bible quotations from other books
available, its influence is so great.**

Let's continue on our backward journey.

(Pick up the string and attach picture of Jesus on the cross.)

The last series of events in the Bible concern the life, work and
effect of Jesus Christ. He was a man of the Bible, but was he a
man of history?

Well, if he wasn't for real, then history tells us that an awful lot
of people died horrible deaths professing faith in an imaginary
person.

Some of them knew Jesus personally, or knew someone who knew him. A lot of their stories come to us from other books, such as those by the Roman historians, Tacitus and Pliny, who would have no reason to lie to us. There is also plenty of evidence that Jesus existed from Roman and Jewish sources outside the Bible. In fact, **no serious scholar these days denies that Jesus lived.**

(Attach picture of Old Testament theme, then leave the ball of string on the Bible.)

But what of the **Old** Testament (the first part of the Bible that is used by Jews), with its tales of brutality, love, hate, sacrifice, natural disasters, miracles and general mayhem? Do we accept this as history, too? The fact is that a lot of it is **actual** history, again confirmed by other sources, writing about the to-ing and fro-ing of the ancient empires of Babylon and Assyria, for example. Archaeology and even modern science have proved time and time again the accuracy of events in the Old Testament.

You may remember the story of Jericho. Joshua blew the trumpet and the walls came tumbling down. Well, when they were digging up the ancient city in 1930 they discovered that the walls had fallen **outwards**, not inwards like every other ancient city that had been conquered. Strange, but true.

Discussion

Ask people to suggest stories from the Bible that may be historically suspect and discuss each, making use of reference materials if necessary, examining the consequences of them being true. Good examples would be Adam and Eve, the Flood, the Exodus. Of course time will limit the possibility for detailed discussions. (See website for information.)

Presentation

One of the most common attacks on the Bible is to say that this book is so old, and has passed through so many hands, that how can we know that the Bible we read today is the same as the one written all those thousands of years ago? Surely Christians and Jews have added to it and modified it where it suited, to give the impression, for example, that prophecies were added after the thing **actually** happened, if you get the drift.

(Remove the string from the Bible.)

Well, this is quite mistaken.

(Replace the ball of string onto the pages of the Bible.)

Let us first consider the New Testament, which was originally written in Greek. There are, in fact, at least eight times as many surviving manuscripts of the New Testament as for any other ancient documents you may mention, such as Homer's *Iliad*. So we can safely say that the New Testament has come to us as an authentic document. In fact there are **over 24,000 copies of original manuscripts** and, guess what, they **all** agree with each other. The New Testament we read now is **exactly the same** as that originally written nearly 2000 years ago.

(Start wrapping the string around the Bible.)

And what of the Old Testament? If it could be proved that prophecies concerning, say, the coming of Jesus, were fiddled by Christians afterwards, then the whole Bible would come into question. So we can thank the stone-throwing skills of Muhammad, a Bedouin shepherd boy, for providing us with the most amazing confirmation of the Bible ever found. The stone that he threw entered a cave system, just south of Jericho in Israel, shattering pottery as it landed. This was 1947 and a chain of events was to unfold which led to the discovery of the **Dead Sea Scrolls**. One of the scrolls discovered was a complete manuscript of the Book of Isaiah in the Old Testament. This manuscript was found to be 1000 years older than any other Isaiah manuscript and, importantly, dated before the coming of Jesus. This document was almost identical to the text of Isaiah that we know from our Bibles.

Pottery-shattering gives way to earth-shattering, because that was the effect of this discovery, described as the greatest manuscript discovery of modern times.

(Pick up Bible.)

So, those were the facts. Just a few key pointers to get you thinking about a book that, if you're honest, has probably made less impact on your life than the latest John Grisham, Stephen King or even Harry Potter. Give it some thought, and, if you're intrigued and motivated, you can always give it a once-over. Available in all good bookshops, libraries and hotel rooms.

Challenge

Find out for yourself how the Bible has influenced society. Pick up a daily newspaper and see how may references you can find to Bible stories (even if in jest), or even Bible verses. See if you can find a family Bible, perhaps at your grandparents' house. If you do, look for inscriptions or comments. It will show you how earlier generations have used this book and may give you some insights into some of your relatives and the way they lived.

Parting shot

The Bible is a book that you just can't ignore. Why not pick one up and read one of the smaller sections – how about the story of Jonah in the book of that name?

Useful resources

http://www.77talksforteens.com/talk15.htm

16
Live For Today, Die Tomorrow?

Theme

A challenge to today's lifestyle. Investigating how we live our lives today and how we can open ourselves to the possibility of a spiritual element.

Preparation

OHP/flip chart.

Presentation

(Write or pin up on chart.)

"I'd rather be dead than cool." Kurt Cobain, Nirvana.

"It's not that I'm afraid to die. I just don't want to be there when it happens." Woody Allen.

"Be happy while you're living, for you're a long time dead." Scottish proverb.

"Live as if you were to die tomorrow. Learn as if you were to live for ever." Gandhi.

"Live for today for tomorrow we die" Anon.

If you had to pick one as your motto, which would you choose? *(Ask for a show of hands.)*

The **four themes** here are:

- Fear of the act of dying.
- Making the most of life.
- Living a worthy live.
- Living selfishly with no fear of the future.

The question is: what is the purpose of life?

Either *(write on chart)*:

- **Today** people. Live for the present with no thought of the future – physically or spiritually. Are happy, having fun, clubbing, carefree, smoking, drinking, drugs, sex.
- **Tomorrow** people. Live for the future, making provisions, physically or spiritually. Look after body, healthy lifestyle, drug-free, celibate, teetotal, religious search.

You can be **both**, of course, having bits of each.

Do you mainly live as a today person or a tomorrow person? Society teaches you how to be **today** people.

- Sex is acceptable – avoid AIDS and pregnancy through condoms, rather than self-control. And if pregnancy comes – there's still abortion!
- Drugs are allowed to a certain degree – ecstacy and cannabis are rife, despite their damage to heath.
- Cigarettes – still cool, lung cancer is for when you're old!
- Drinking – socially acceptable despite deaths through lack of control, alcoholism.

This is not a lecture on your nasty habits – I just want to highlight that living for today has **consequences for tomorrow**.

In our group we ought to be concerned about being **tomorrow** people.

It really is cool to live a long healthy life, so you might as well do what you can now to help that happen!

And being a "Christian" group here, we are mostly concerned about your inner life, the bit of you that is **really** you and the bit of you that is the most neglected.

"Death is for old people!"

Is it? Plenty of people die young, and what have they done to prepare themselves for it?

In fact, if you're a fully-fledged **today** person – smoking, drinking, drug-taking, sleeping around, etc – this day may come sooner than you think.

We're not asking you to get all morbid, just be open to possibilities.

Discussion

Is there life after death? Do we care – if not, why not? Is there heaven and hell? *(Don't preach, just let them discuss and encourage them to think about these things.)*

Parting shot

We can all die tomorrow and, if so, do we really know where we're going?

Useful resources

http://www.77talksforteens.com/talk16.htm

Thinking Clearly about Life after Death, Graham H. Twelftree (Monarch)

17
By Their Fruits . . .

Theme

By describing a true story of Christian sacrifice we seek to show that there are Christians who are serious enough about their faith to make the ultimate sacrifice for others.

Preparation

OHP/flip chart.

Presentation

Sacrifice. *(Write word on chart.)*

We hear a lot of this word.

- Go on, make a sacrifice, take your wife out instead of going to the game.
- Those suicide bombers made the ultimate sacrifice and killed 20 others at the same time.

But the purest, most authentic use of this word is to describe an act whereby someone gives up their life **in order to save others**.

Here is a story about five Christian missionaries who, in 1955, ventured into the jungles of Ecuador to spread the Gospel to a tribe, the savage Auca Indians, who had previously been untouched by outside contact.

These men were Jim Elliot, Pete Fleming, Nate Saint, Ed McCully and Roger Youderian. They secretly made plans to make contact with the tribe and one day, Saint saw an Auca village from his aeroplane. From September to January, he flew his plane over the spot and dropped gifts from a basket to the Indians. They made a camp on a small strip of land and on 6 January a man and a woman of the tribe came to meet the five missionaries. The missionaries welcomed them and talked to them using memorised Auca phrases. Saint gave the man a ride in his aeroplane. Then the two went back to their village.

On 8 January 1956, Nate flew over the village and noticed that no men were in sight. He radioed his wife who was at the missionary base and told her that they were hoping for visitors at 2.30 p.m. and that he would call again at 4.35 p.m. At the given time, his wife waited for his call but heard nothing. A plane was sent to investigate. It reported that Nate's plane was demolished and four bodies were found in the river. They could not find McCully's body, but they did find one of his shoes. All five men had been speared to death by the hostile tribe. The bodies were already decomposing and they could only identify them by the objects in their pockets. They buried the remains in a common grave on the beach.

So that's the story. Sad and pointless, it seems.

Discussion

How would you feel if you were the wives of these missionaries? The wives were Christians too.

Presentation

But the story doesn't end.

Believe it or not, following her husband's death, Elisabeth Elliot decided to resume his work with the Auca Indians.

She and her daughter, Valerie, moved to Ecuador and in following years, further contacts were made with the Auca tribes. Rachel Saint, another of the widows, worked with her.

In 1959, Rachel Saint, Elisabeth and Valerie moved in with **the same Auca tribe who killed the five men**. They studied their language and worked on translations.

Later, Jim Elliot's killers and other members of the tribe were converted to Christianity. They explained to the women that the Auca man who first came into contact with the white men reported that he thought the intention of the missionaries was to eat the Aucas. So they had killed them in self-defence!

Gikita, the Auca who led the attack against the five missionaries, testified: "God says now you are forgiven. And I know I'm forgiven for all these spearings. I'm going to meet Nate Saint in heaven some day. And we'll just wrap our arms around each other and be happy."

Discussion

Could you have carried on this work with the very people who had killed your loved ones? What does this say about their faith?

Presentation

Elisabeth's son, Steve, also became a missionary, following in his father's and mother's footsteps. One day he met an elderly Auca Indian called "Grandfather", who said to him, "I am one of the men who killed Jim, Nate and his friends that day in 1956. But since that time, I have come to follow God's carvings. We have learned his markings now and we follow his trails."

From that day on, these two men, killer and victim, worked together to tell the story of how God had worked and is still working all things together for his ultimate will.

During a lecture in America, "Grandfather" made an interesting comment on the Columbine school massacre in the USA, when some schoolkids went on a killing frenzy.

"When I heard of what had happened at Columbine High School here in America and how those young boys killed other students, I said to myself, 'We were savages like this too before we came to know the carvings of Jesus. We too killed each other until we came to follow his trails.'"

This man of no formal education and no civilisation stood before this crowd of well-do-do Americans and called them "savages".

He continued. "A group of American students came to us in Ecuador to do a story on our tribe and when they got there and were with us for some time, they asked us where the savages were. We explained to them that it was we; we were the savages that they had come to see. They were amazed that we were no longer killing each other and that we were living in peace and harmony. How is it that these students were amazed at our transformed lives? Isn't that what the power of God is supposed to do, transform your life?"

Discussion

What can we learn from this "Grandfather"? Who are the real savages?

Parting shot

When have you done something that has been a real sacrifice, where someone else has gained from your actions, without any gain for yourself?

Useful resources

http://www.77talksforteens.com/talk17.htm

18
To Whom Do We Turn?

Theme

How major world events can turn one's life upside down. Taking 11 September 2001 as a starting point, we look at our need for meaning and comfort, when the world seems not to make sense any more. A gentle introduction to the Bible.

Preparation

OHP/flip chart to illustrate points. Newspaper clippings depicting world disasters and acts of terrorism, with particular emphasis on World Trade Center attack. A Bible (slightly doctored – see later).

Presentation

(Show picture of WTC terrorist attack.)

Where were you on 11 September 2001? *(Or any subsequent event of similar impact.)*

Discussion

What effect did it have on your life, our country, the world? *(Note them on chart.)*

Isn't it incredible that an act by a handful of people can have such far-reaching results on so many levels?

Whom do we turn to when something happens that we are not equipped to deal with on a personal level?

- Do we look outwards to politicians, scientists, teachers, family?
- Do we turn inwards to our own resources?
- Do we just shrug our shoulders and get on with it?
- Do we look for some deeper meaning, in a religious sense?

(Ask for a show of hands.)

Whom do we really trust to explain these things to us, show us the way? *(Ask for a show of hands, working from the same list as above.)*

Whom can we really trust, then?

- Do politicians tell us the whole story?
- How impartial is the media?
- Can we trust family and friends to advise, or are they out of their depth?
- Can we trust ourselves to reach informed conclusions?

Wouldn't life be easier if we had a blueprint for living, a guide that could explain the workings of the world, but could also provide clear personal guidelines for us as individuals? If such a blueprint existed, whom would we trust to create it?

Presentation

This may be an obvious point to make, particularly as this is a **Christian** group, but this blueprint does exist. But even then, it's not that straightforward.

(Hold a Bible up.)

This book has motivated acts of mercy, love, self-sacrifice. *(Give examples relevant to the group – Martin Luther King, Mother Teresa, William Wilberforce, etc. See website for information.)*

(Turn the Bible over – on the back a sign "HANDLE WITH CARE" is attached to it.)

But there's a downside.

This book has motivated acts of hate, murder, vengeance, even greed. *(Give examples – David Koresh, Crusades, Jim Jones, Moonies, some TV evangelists, etc.)*

So what right do we have to hold this up as our "blueprint for living"?

We have a perfect right because we acknowledge the health warning. It's no good just opening it, reading something and saying "Thus spake the Lord". *(Give demonstration.)*

We need the **hidden** ingredient.

A motorbike, a car, a train, an aeroplane – these are just deadly weapons in the hands of a person without the training.

Same with the Bible. We need to be trained to use it. I'm not **necessarily** talking about being told by someone else to read it.

We need the author **himself** to guide us. The one who created the blueprint. That's the hidden ingredient and there I will rest my case for now.

Parting shot

If the Bible really contains words from God himself, don't you think that God will also show the sincere reader exactly how to understand it?

Useful resources

http://www.77talksforteens.com/talk18.htm

19
Who's the Daddy?

Theme

When we say that God is in charge of the world, sometimes we
need to show exactly what we mean. We explore the idea that
everything in nature is under God's dominion, to counter the
New Age idea of "Mother Earth".

Preparation

OHP/flip chart. A globe (or world map) – even better would be a
poster of the famous Apollo 8 Earthrise photograph. Either a
lady's hat or a picture of a lady's hat (with some Blu Tack). Bible.

Presentation

In December 1968 an important picture was taken. It was
taken by astronauts on the Apollo 8 mission and was of the
planet Earth rising above the barren lunar landscape. It was the
first photograph of Earth from space and was to have a major
affect on the way mankind saw itself.

The American poet Archibald MacLeish wrote these words a
few days later. *(Display on chart.)*

"Earth was no longer the world but a small, wet, spinning
planet in the solar system of a minor star off at the edge of an
inconsiderable galaxy in the immeasurable distances of space.
To see Earth as it truly is, small and blue and beautiful in that
eternal silence where it floats, is to see ourselves as riders on the
Earth together, brothers on the bright loveliness in that eternal
cold – brothers who know they are truly brothers."

One week after the astronauts had returned to Earth, all the world's media featured the Earthrise photo very prominently. It became the most important symbol of the new environmental movement (we now call them the "Greens"). This photo led to fresh scientific views of our planet and its place within the universe.

(Write the word "Gaia" on chart.)

Q: Has anyone heard of this word?
A: It is the Greek goddess of the Earth.
Q: Has anyone heard it used lately in relation to popular beliefs about the environment?
A: The Gaia Hypothesis.

The Gaia Hypothesis. Formulated by British scientist, James Lovelock, partly as a result of the Earthrise photo, in the late 1960s. It states that the whole Earth itself **is a living being**, able to respond to external events, such as man's destruction of the environment.

This has been linked with the ancient concept of **Mother Earth** or **Mother Nature**.

(If you have a globe, add the hat to it. If you are displaying a map or photo, then attach the picture of the hat.)

The thinking goes something like this.

Just as different parts of our body are needed to make the whole function, and just as the ability of the whole body to function properly is weakened when one part is hurt or damaged, so the various parts of our environment (the ecosystem) – air, water, plants, animals, human beings, etc. – need to work together to make the whole function as a healthy living body. Because human beings have become alienated from

Gaia – Mother Earth – we are polluting the earth and thus damaging our own body. So we must urgently rediscover the sacred both in nature and in ourselves before we destroy the planet.

Now this may seem a ridiculous idea to some, but to others it may make sense. It's a strange idea, but some people find it an attractive idea. But is it correct?

Discussion

Bear in mind the fact that the primary motivation of living beings is self-preservation. If the Earth is a living being, what do you think Mother Earth thinks of mankind, considering what we have done to the planet? Are we a friend or enemy? If an enemy, what would her expected response to us be?

Presentation

The Christian view is **very** different.

God is creator of the universe, ourselves and the Earth. It says so in the first ten words of the Bible. *(Open Bible and read out Genesis 1:1, then close it.)*

And that's the Christian view. It's not just there at the beginning, it appears again and again all through the book. God wants to make sure we know **who's the Daddy**.

(Point in turn at map/globe and Bible.) Mother Earth, Father God. Goes together well, doesn't it. A good match?

No, it's certainly **not** a match made in heaven, because it is not true. "Mother" Earth, like us, is a **creation** of God, not equal to him. But this doesn't give us an excuse to treat the Earth with disrespect.

Discussion

If God created the Earth what do you think he feels about what we have done to the earth with pollution, destruction of the rainforests, etc?

Presentation

God **does** care about what we have done to the environment.

Our problem is not that we are alienated from Mother Earth but, rather, that we are alienated from Father God, with our failure to take care of the Earth in the way God commanded us to in the Bible.

(Read Psalm 8.)

Let's contrast the two positions and decide which is the more reasonable.

- **Mother Earth** is an uncaring, angry and ancient being, having lived for ages in peace and harmony until mankind, fuelled by scientific endeavour and greed for natural resources, has unthinkingly attacked her. Her revenge is manifested in earthquakes, severe weather and other natural disasters, with much more promised in the future.
- **Father God** has put us in charge of the natural world but we have blown it. Natural disasters are, in the main, due to our selfish actions, such as the destruction of the ozone layer and of the rainforests.

So Christians can be "Green". Although the environmental movement – Greenpeace, Friends of the Earth, etc. – is not a Christian movement, Christianity **is** concerned about the environment, because God cares for Earth, his creation.

Parting shot

Which would you prefer, a selfish mother or a loving father?

Useful resources

http://www.77talksforteens.com/talk19.htm

20
Imagine We Give Peace a Chance

Theme

An analysis of the music and philosophy of John Lennon, concentrating on the influential song "Imagine" and looking at the concept of peace and how humanity has never found it and is never likely to, if left to its own devices.

Preparation

OHP/flip chart. Copy of "Imagine" by John Lennon if possible (with words on chart – words can be found on the website.)

Presentation

Who remembers the Beatles? Too young – don't know what you've missed. They were supremely talented songwriters and musicians and, almost single-handedly, defined the 1960s. John Lennon recently made the Top Ten of the BBC's "most influential Britons" in history.

But it wasn't all good innocent fun.

John Lennon, the most vocal member of the group, was a peace activist and a humanist (i.e. he was non-religious).

In 1971 he wrote a song that in many subsequent polls worldwide has been voted among the most influential and important songs ever written – "Imagine".

(Play song or at least display lyrics – and get them to sing it unaccompanied.)

Discussion

Discuss these lyrics, with particular emphasis on whether people think that the ideals expressed are attainable – perhaps conduct a vote on the matter.

Presentation

The summary of the lyrics:

1. Wouldn't things be better without religion, or a heaven or hell?
2. Wouldn't things be better without national boundaries?
3. Wouldn't things be better if we shared all our resources?

Although we agree with the third point (although John was not exactly known for sharing **his** resources – in fact his estate is so money hungry that the cost of reproducing the lyrics of "Imagine" in this book would have been astronomical) and are not equipped to discuss the second, what John Lennon doesn't offer is a **solution**, hence the title of the song . . . "Imagine".

What he's implying is that we're really incapable of these lofty goals . . . but it's OK to dream, to imagine.

But what if . . . it wasn't just a dream?

Lennon implies that religion is the **problem** – suggesting that if we just lived for today, without hoping for heaven, or fearing a hell – the world would be a better place.

But perhaps religion, or specifically Christianity, could be the **solution**?

(Write the following words on the chart.)

"They shall beat their swords into ploughshares, and their spears into pruning hooks; nation shall not lift up sword against nation; neither shall they learn war any more."

Q: Does anyone know where these words come from and on which famous building they can be found?
A: In Isaiah – Old Testament of the Bible. Inscribed on the United Nations building in New York.

These religious words are on a building which takes not a religious approach, but a human approach to the problems of the world. On its fiftieth anniversary the United Nations organisation issued a statement that said:

(Write the following words on the chart.)

"These words from Isaiah will never be more than an ideal for humanity. If, in our service as United Nations peacekeepers, we can help make that ideal more true than false, more promising than distant, more able to protect the innocent than embolden the guilty, we will have done our part."

They too are imagining – they realise that they will never be able to reach this ideal.

But when Isaiah wrote these words, he wasn't referring to a United Nations, or any other group of people. You see, the United Nations was only **partially** quoting from the verse. This is the full verse.

(Write the following words on the chart.)

"He will judge between the nations, and will settle disputes for many peoples. They will beat their swords into ploughshares, and their spears into pruning hooks. Nation will not take up sword against nation, nor will they learn war any more."

Ah ha, it's a person that's being referred to here. It's also referring to some time in the future. That person is not in the world . . . yet. But he is coming soon.

This is a core belief in the Christian faith – about a third of all Bible prophecy refers to this event – the return of Jesus Christ.

Only then will the world know true and everlasting peace.

But . . . until then, we, as individuals, can know peace. *(Read John 14:27.)*

Discussion

Our world is very uncertain and insecure.

- What would you give to have true peace – an assurance that, whatever happens in the world, or to you individually, you can rise above it with real hope?
- If you had this peace, would it free you to do things that you wouldn't otherwise feel able to do?

Parting shot

Is there true peace in your heart? Would you like to have it?

Useful resources

http://www.77talksforteens.com/talk20.htm

21
The Full Story?

Theme

An investigation on how we form our opinions. How do we filter through the mass of information that comes at us from all angles? On what basis do we formulate views? Offer the Bible as a trustworthy guide to life.

Preparation

OHP/flip chart, Bible.

Presentation

One hour after the terrorist attack on the World Trade Center, New York, 11 September 2001, a senior advisor to an English politician distributed an e-mail to associates. It suggested that, because of the anticipated media overload, this would be a good time to "bury" any embarrassing news stories, as no one would notice. What amazing insensitive cynicism, we may say, but let's see . . .

How many people here mainly read the tabloid newspapers (red-tops), and how many mainly read the broadsheets? *(Ask for a show of hands.)*

Q: How many messages a day do you think you receive on average?
A: A recent study indicated that the average Westerner is bombarded with more than 4000 messages a day, from e-mails to washing instructions on clothes. Travelling to work can expose you to 150 messages – billboards, newspaper

headlines, etc. A trip to the supermarket can expose you to over 1,500 messages!

Discussion

Using the chart, discuss the major newspapers and note down the usual editorial line taken by each paper – who reads it? Is it:

- Supportive of existing government
- Critical of existing government
- Liberal
- Authoritarian
- Preachy
- Trashy
- Serious
- Influential?

Also think about other major news sources: TV, satellite TV, internet, news magazines.

Presentation

Q: How did people receive the news of national and world events in the nineteenth century?
A: Newspaper only.

People read just one newspaper rather than the many news sources available to us now.

Discussion

How much do you think our views are affected by which newspaper we read, or which TV station we watch? Are we helped by having so many options, or does it confuse us?

Presentation

At the time of the World Trade Center attack, the following events were also happening.

- Foot and Mouth disease was still a major problem in the UK.
- Thousands of Christians were murdered by the Sudanese government.
- Massacre of Indonesian Christians by Muslims.
- Continuing unrest in Zimbabwe.
- Thousands of deaths from AIDS in Southern Africa.

None of these featured in our daily papers on 12 September. Just because a news story gains extensive coverage, it doesn't mean that other events just ceased to be – it is just that media editors decide what we should read that day.

It is hard to formulate independent opinions when faced with so many editorials and commentators. Wouldn't it be good if we had a dependable yardstick to help us to figure out what is going on?

But who can we trust?

This book! *(Show Bible.)*

(Read Hebrews 4:12–13)

Not just grand words, but a reality for any Christian. This doesn't mean you can just pick this up and know the answer to everything. It doesn't work like that.

But be honest – whatever your current view – wouldn't it be great if one book **did** have all the answers?

You don't stick a learner driver into a 747 cockpit and expect him to pilot the plane! Training is needed, help is needed.

Training and help is provided free to anyone who is sincerely looking for the author of this book. If you want help reading this, then just ask him, but be prepared for an unexpected, exciting, life-changing journey.

Challenge

Get hold of a Bible during the week, from a library or borrow one from the youth group. Alternatively the website will give links to on-line Bibles. Just pick a short section, say a couple of paragraphs. Read it a couple of times, then think about it. Challenge God to bring the words alive to you. There's nothing to lose, but you owe it to yourself to at least give it a try. Report back next week. All we ask for is honesty and openness.

Parting shot

Are you independent and free-thinking enough to pick up a book that is largely ridiculed by today's society and give it a chance to speak to you?

Useful resources

http://www.77talksforteens.com/talk21.htm

22
Moral Fibre and
Other Loose Threads

Theme

With illustrations from real life, this is an examination of
today's society with an emphasis on moral education and how
ethical standards have been on a gradual decline as Christianity
has lost its grip on our nation.

Preparation

None.

Presentation

On 19 October 2001, two stories appeared in a popular daily
newspaper. Listen and see what you can find in common to
them both.

"A suicide note was found by the bodies of a couple who had
just celebrated their fiftieth wedding anniversary – it read 'The
cause of death of my wife and myself has been the anti-social
behaviour of our neighbour's children and their friends and the
total lack of consideration of their parents as to the distress
they have caused . . . this has led to our decision that we no
longer wish to be part of a society that allows this situation to
reach this point and we feel we would be better off out of it.'"

"Last night a bunch of kids represented Chelsea football club
in their game in Tel Aviv, Israel. Meanwhile six of Chelsea's
hugely-paid and cosseted star international players were sitting
at home in London, watching the match on TV. They had been

given the option of pulling out – because of the deteriorating international situation – and did so. . . . There was as much danger at that match as sitting in a dentist's waiting room, yet today those six players will be shopping at Harrods and lunching at The Ivy. Obviously life must go on (Chelsea lost 2–0)."

Q: What do these stories have in common?
A: Selfish, uncaring, self-seeking behaviour.

We can call this lack of **moral fibre**.

Let's go on a historical journey, to see how we have reached where we are.

In 1914, Britain went to war against Germany in the First World War. Men between the ages of 18 and 41 went to war – not always cheerfully – but most went, to fight for their country. It was a dirty war. Many died, horribly.

Discussion

If you were called up to a Third World War and a possible gory death, would your sense of patriotism and community overcome your cowardice? Would you go to war? Would you sacrifice yourself for your nation, your family? If not, why not?

Presentation

The Second World War came along 20 years after the First World War. Again most young men went to war, even though they knew what had happened to the cream of youth in the First World War. But a sense of duty and the knowledge that this was a war of survival against the Nazi menace ensured that they went.

Discussion

Would you go to war against a foe who would otherwise
destroy your nation and possibly kill your family? What would
you fight for?

Presentation

After the war things changed. In the 1950s families started
getting richer and a new type of person appeared.

The teenager!

The teenager was invented in the 1950s by marketing men
looking for new people to buy their products. Before the 1950s,
you were a kid until you were 21, then you became an adult. In
the 1950s, there was suddenly a "middle bit". You **are** that
middle bit!

You were given rock 'n' roll, Coca Cola, Levi jeans. Then you
were given the Beatles, discos, Pepsi Cola, MacDonalds, Nikes,
punk rock, Britney Spears and Harry Potter.

You have everything you've ever asked for, and not asked for!

But would you fight for it?

Discussion

So returning to our Chelsea footballers – do you think they
would go to war, if our country needed them to?

And what about the teenage thugs who sent those pensioners
over the edge to suicide?

Presentation

What has changed since the 1940s? Perhaps there's an answer in a comment by Cormac Murphy O'Connor, the head of the Catholic Church in England, in September 2001:

"It does seem in our country, in Britain today, that Christianity as a sort of background to people's lives and moral decisions and to the government, and the social life of the country, has now almost been vanquished."

Parting shot

Without the Highway Code – a given set of rules of the road – there would be confusion and mayhem. What would happen to our society if all the rules for civilised living disappeared?

Useful resources

http://www.77talksforteens.com/talk22.htm

MELLOW YELLOW SECTION

Finding Answers

23
Wouldn't It Be Nice?

Theme

What the Christian life offers and what it doesn't offer.

Preparation

OHP/flip chart, series of photographs, posters, etc, copy of "Footprints".

Presentation

Wouldn't it be nice if you were . . .

(Show picture of a superhero, or superman – or superman with face of a mutual acquaintance superimposed.)

Indestructible!

Q: What would you do if you were indestructible?
A: Dangerous sports, walk into war zones and "take out" the villains?

Well, we can't offer you that.

(Show picture of an upper class toff, preferably in a drunken state.)

What about a guaranteed easy life – no worries or upsets – just three score and ten years of fun, fun, fun?

Q: Would you like a life with no uncertainties?
A: Boring? Predictable? Safe? Liberating?

We can't offer you that either, I'm afraid.

(Show picture of Churchill or Second World War.)

On 10 May 1940, Winston Churchill became Prime Minister at a key point in the Second World War. When he met his Cabinet on 13 May he told them, "I have nothing to offer but blood, toil, tears and sweat."

He didn't mince his words. Neither did Jesus.

It's not meant to be easy.

Jesus said: "Anyone who does not take up his cross and follow me is not worthy of me."

(Show picture of Jesus on cross.)

Jesus died horribly on the cross. Most of his friends also died. And not in nice ways. Crucified upside down, beheaded, stoned, clubbed, hacked to death, speared, shot by arrows, flayed alive and boiled alive.

They were ordinary people like you and me, but something got them through it because all of them, Jesus included, could have escaped death by the three simple words . . . "I was wrong".

But they didn't.

Polycarp was a second-generation Christian living in the second century. He was a bishop. The Romans captured him and led him into a stadium. In front of thousands he was asked to deny his faith and swear by the spirit of Caesar. He faced the crowds and said: "Four score and six years (86 years) have I been Jesus' servant and he has done me no wrong. How then can I blaspheme my king who saved me?"

He was burnt at the stake and impaled with a sword.

Three simple words. "I was wrong . . ." but instead he chose a grisly death. Something must have got him through it.

Christians have died such deaths over the past 2000 years. These days there are over 150,000 Christian martyrs every year – that's over 400 a day – one every three minutes or so, which means that *(enter number)* have already died since we started this talk.

What gets them through it? **Who** gets them through it?

It might be useful to read out the famous "Footprints" piece, as seen on greeting cards, china mugs, Christian T shirts, etc. as it illustrates the next point.

Now we're not all called to be martyrs, but again we're not going to be wrapped up in cotton wool.

Jesus told his closest followers, "I have told you these things, so that in me you may have peace. In this world you will have trouble. But take heart! I have overcome the world" (John 16:33).

The point of the Christian life is not that you escape from disease, tragedies, acts of violence, earthquakes or war.

Many Christians died in the World Trade Center, in the Second World War and in every major tragedy you've heard of in the Western world.

The point of the Christian life is that Jesus gets you through it, he doesn't help you to avoid it!

Jesus said, "Come to me, all you who are weary and burdened, and I will give you rest. Take my yoke upon you and learn from me, for I am gentle and humble in heart, and you will find rest for your souls. For my yoke is easy and my burden is light" (Matthew 11:28).

Christians live in the same world as everyone else. They don't escape from the bad stuff. They are just helped through it.

When all those people died – and are still dying – as martyrs for their Christian faith, you can trust me . . . they were not alone.

Discussion

If Christianity promised you supernatural protection from the world and its problems, what sort of religion do you think it would be, and what sort of people would it attract?

Parting shot

What is more important, an easy life or a guaranteed after-life?

Useful resources

http://www.77talksforteens.com/talk23.htm

24
A Truly Historical Book.
Part 1: A Tale of Two Cities

Theme

One accusation thrown at the Bible, in regard to the
prophetic, is that it was written **after** the historic "fulfilment"
of the prophecy. This study focuses on key prophecies in
the Book of Isaiah and how, in the light of the Dead Sea
Scroll findings, a complete copy of Isaiah has been found
pre-dating Jesus by over a century! This fact will serve to
focus the mind more on these prophecies and their historic
fulfilment.

Preparation

OHP/flip chart. Map of ancient world. Current picture of
Petra. Bibles distributed to all.

Presentation

(Hold up a Bible.)

Q: How old is this book?
A: What we have is an English translation of texts originally
written mostly in Hebrew and Greek, which date back to
the fifth to the ninth century.
Q: Does that mean that the Bible was written centuries after
the depicted events?
A: No, the Bible was written over a period from around
1500 BC onwards, but it wasn't compiled into one complete
book until many centuries later.
Q: So there's a chance that, when the Bible speaks about events

that hadn't happened yet, it could have been written **after** these events had occurred?

A: No. If the Bible were a book written and organised by us fallible humans, then there **would** be a chance that such trickeries could have taken place, but the Bible has but one author – God – and, such is his character, he would never trick us or lie to us.

Then you would say that, wouldn't you?

And I **do** say that, and I **can** back it up.

(Write "Dead Sea Scrolls" on chart.)

Who has heard of this?

In 1947, in a cave near the Dead Sea, a shepherd boy happened to find jars containing old leather rolls. He did not know what they were, and sold them for next to nothing. Eventually archaeologists heard about the find and where it had been made. Between them, shepherds and archaeologists collected pieces of over 400 rolls. These books belonged to the library of a religious commune at Qumran, on the edge of the Dead Sea. Their owners had hidden them in caves when the Roman army advanced against the rebel Jews in AD 68. The dry heat of the region preserved them. Old Testament books were favourites in the library. Every one of them is there, except the Book of Esther.

We are just going to look at one book – the Book of Isaiah in the Old Testament.

In the Dead Sea Scrolls they found a complete book of Isaiah. They dated it scientifically and found that it was 1000 years older than any other known copy of Isaiah – it was, in fact, dated to over 100 years before the time of Jesus.

Q: What is the significance of this?

A: This meant that any prophecy mentioned in Isaiah concerning events that were to occur after around 125 BC, could **not** have been altered after the event it referred to – because the book had already been written!

This is significant. Today we are going to look at some prophecies made in Isaiah that fit into that category.

We are going to look at two ancient cities, Petra and Babylon.

First, Petra. *(Show picture of the modern city if you can.)* Has anyone been there?

Petra was the capital of Edom, a region that covers part of modern-day Jordan. It was an evil kingdom, constantly a thorn in God's side in Old Testament times, through its treatment of Israel.

Consequently God made a proclamation against Edom in Isaiah 34:5–15 *(Read)*. He clearly didn't like them too much!

Verse 10: "It will lie desolate; no one will ever pass through it again." There have been no permanent inhabitants of Edom and Petra, since Roman times. No attempt has ever been made to re-establish a state or city. Until the late nineteenth century there were no roads in the region at all and only the occasional historian made his way there to report the devastation and desolation of the area. There are still no through highways to this day, although hundreds of tourists enter Petra to view the 'rose-red city', so called because of its distinctive russet-coloured rock faces.

Verses 13–15: "a place for animals". The place now swarms with scorpions and is a home for lizards, vipers, eagles and owls.

Alexander Keith, the explorer, said, in 1861, "I would that the sceptic could stand as I did, among the ruins of this city among the rocks and there open the sacred book and read the words of the inspired penman, written when this desolate place was one of the greatest cities of the world . . . I see his cheeks pale, his lip quivering and his heart quaking with fear, as the ruined city cries out to him . . ."

Next, Babylon. *(Show ancient map for location.)*

The capital of one of the largest ancient empires. It covered 196 square miles, with 250 watchtowers.

Isaiah 13:19–22 *(Read.)*

A similar fate to Petra and Edom. Now just ruins – it was excavated in the nineteenth century by Germans. Until recently, Saddam Hussein was supposed to be rebuilding there, but events overtook him.

Challenge

Some say that of course these ancient cities have been destroyed, but what about Rome, Damascus, Jerusalem, Athens – all in the Bible but all thriving. Encourage students to read Ezekiel 26:1–21 (Tyre), Ezekiel 28:22–23 (Sidon), Nahum 1–3 (Nineveh) and contrast with Jeremiah 31:38–40 (Jerusalem).

Parting shot

How much proof do you need before you start believing in possibilities?

Useful resources

http://www.77talksforteens.com/talk24.htm

25
A Truly Historical Book.
Part 2: A Tale of Two People

Theme

Following our look at prophetic passages in Isaiah, our
attention turns to the "suffering servant" passage in Isaiah 53
and it is compared to the life and death of Jesus.

Preparation

OHP/flip chart. Bibles distributed to all.

Presentation

We discovered last week that, due to the finding of the Dead
Sea Scrolls, we can be absolutely sure that the Book of Isaiah
was written over 100 years before the coming of Jesus Christ.

Which is handy because it is **his** life that we will be examining
today.

*(Assign two people as Bible readers. One will read from Isaiah
53, the other from the Gospels. Get them to stand either side of
the chart and read aloud when prompted.)*

(Read Isaiah 53:1–3, John 1:10–11.)

(Write on chart "despised and rejected".)

(Read Isaiah 53:4–6, John 19:33–37.)

(Write on chart "stricken by God".)

(Read Isaiah 53:7, John 19:8–10.)

(Write on chart "led meekly to his death".)

(Read Isaiah 53:8–9, John 19:38–42.)

(Write on chart "cut off in his prime".)

(Read Isaiah 53:10–11, Luke 22:39–44.)

(Write on chart "carried out the will of God".)

(Read Isaiah 53:12, Luke 22:35–37.)

(Write on chart "died for a purpose".)

You will agree there are uncanny similarities. The Book of Isaiah was written around 800 years before the time of Jesus and, even if some people may dispute this, we know with certainty, thanks to the Dead Sea Scrolls, that the latest this book could have been written was **over 100 years before Jesus**. Yet it really seems to be talking about Jesus, doesn't it?

Discussion

- How many of these prophecies could Jesus have intentionally fulfilled out of "messianic zeal"? Could he have manipulated events around him to bring about these fulfilments?
- If he was a charlatan and an impostor, would he have willingly gone to a painful death?
- How come his disciples didn't fully understand what he was doing – surely they, too, would have been familiar with Isaiah 53?

Parting shot

How much proof do you need before you start believing in
possibilities? (Repeated from last week.)

Useful resources

http://www.77talksforteens.com/talk25.htm

26
A Truly Historical Book.
Part 3: A Tale of a Race

Theme

Concluding our look at prophetic passages in Isaiah, our attention now turns to prophecies concerning the Jewish people, with particular reference to their return to the land given to Abraham, Isaac and Jacob.

Preparation

OHP/flip chart, Bibles distributed to all.

Presentation

(Write the following names randomly over the chart: Assyrians, Chaldeans, Hittites, Edomites, Ammonites, Amalekites, Canaanites.)

Q: They've all got one thing in common – what is it?
A: They're all history!

These were all tribes around in Bible times and, at different times, they were conquered and either destroyed or absorbed into one empire or another.

(Now write the word "Jews" in the centre of the chart.)

All except this lot. They were around in Bible times, right from the twelfth chapter of the first book (Genesis). But they're still around – don't you find that strange?

They're around **despite** all the people over the last 2000 years – Greeks, Romans, Crusaders, Nazis and Arabs – who have tried to destroy them or absorb them. They're still around. It's a mystery. Yet the Book of Isaiah, which was written when they were still the dominant people in the land, knew what was going to happen.

The book tells us that they were going to be kicked out of the land, but it also tells us that they were going to survive and return to the land. Even if we're cynics and suggest that Isaiah was written at the latest possible time (about 100 BC), it was still written about events that were to happen centuries later.

(Read Isaiah 11:11–12.)

So the Jews would return for the second time. The first time was when the Jews were exiled by the Babylonians, when they travelled to the East (to modern-day Iraq), before returning under the Persians. Yet in these verses we are talking about the return of the "scattered people of Judah (i.e. Jews) from the four quarters of the Earth".

The exile was initiated by the Romans in AD 70, when they conquered Jerusalem and the Jews were scattered everywhere, ending up in places like China, Australia, South Africa, Russia, Argentina and Japan.

Yet, in this (nearly) 2000-year exile they remained as a **distinct people** – totally confounding the normal course of history that says that immigrant populations are eventually absorbed. (Look at the melting pot of races that became the English people during that time, and also the American people.)

Then, in 1948, the nation of Israel was born. Jews returned to Israel from all around the world – and they are still returning.

(Read Isaiah 43:5–6.)

- They came from the West – England, USA, France . . .
- They came from the East – India, China, Iraq . . .
- They came from the North – Russia, Poland, Ukraine . . .
- They came from the South – Ethiopia, South Africa, Yemen . . .

Yet Isaiah spoke of this over 2,700 years earlier.

There's a story of Frederick the Great, a Prussian czar, who asked a holy man to prove the existence of God in one sentence. The holy man replied, "The Jews, sire".

The continued survival of the Jews is a testament to how the promises of God in the Bible endure, despite what the world says or does.

(On a chart display posters/clippings of some of the following: E.T., Jaws, Close Encounters, Jurassic Park, A.I., Minority Report, Star Wars, Funny Girl, West Side Story, Star Trek (first series), Annie Hall, $E = mc^2$, the Atom Bomb, Yehudi Menuhin, Rodgers and Hammerstein, Ben Elton, Nigella Lawson and Venessa Feltz, etc. General theme is a Jewish one.)

And if this prophecy hadn't taken place, none of this lot would have happened!

Discussion

What other explanations can people come up with for the continued existence of the Jewish people, except by accepting that there's been a degree of divine protection? It may be relevant to comment that their existence has not always been a happy one and that God's ways are, at the end of the day, mysterious – but nevertheless a promise is a promise and God clearly has had a purpose in all this.

Parting shot

How much proof do you need before you start believing in possibilities? *(Repeated from last two weeks.)*

Useful resources

http://www.77talksforteens.com/talk26.htm

27
I Don't Want to Worry You, But . . .

Theme

A discussion of our "final destination". The Christian message
is clear cut – it's either one place or the other. The problem is
presenting these facts with sensitivity and certainty.

Preparation

OHP/flip chart.

Presentation

(Start up a chant.)

- Where there's black, there's . . . white.
- Where there's day, there's . . . night.
- Where there's Adam, there's . . . Eve.
- Where there's a Posh, there's a . . . Becks.
- Where there's heaven, there's . . . hell.

(Write "heaven" and "hell" on the chart.)

But do you believe it? Hell, that is. It's not a popular concept.
It's not trendy. It's not nice.

Do we really believe that all non-Christians are going to burn
in eternity, while Christians spend their time in idle leisure,
playing harps and singing the odd hallelujah chorus?

Discussion

Discuss around the following themes:

- What sort of God is going to let some of us go to heaven and the rest burn in hell?
- Sure, hell may be a good place for Hitler or Jack the Ripper, but not for my dear aunt who died a Buddhist?
- How can a God of love send anyone to hell, no matter how bad he was?

Presentation

Let's turn our thoughts around and ponder this.

Visualise a group of lemmings plummeting over a cliff. You're standing next to them with a fishing net. Every now and again you catch one in your net and save it.

In the same way, rather than looking at God sending all Christians to heaven, why don't we look at him saving them from hell?

The fact is that the whole human race is bound for hell to start with.

That's the consequence of what's called original sin – Adam and Eve and all that.

Mankind has lost the natural right to be face to face with God. It's a difficult one to understand – and this is not the time to explain it – it's just one of those certainties.

- Water flows downwards.
- The toast always lands butter side down.
- Australia wins at sports.
- Mankind deserves to go to hell.

Let's see the black and white of it.

(Read 2 Thessalonians 1:5–10 – written to Christians.)

It makes uncomfortable reading – but just because we feel uncomfortable it doesn't make it wrong.

- Wasp stings are uncomfortable.
- Income tax is uncomfortable.
- Homelessness makes us feel uncomfortable.
- Everlasting destruction in hell makes us feel very uncomfortable.

Of course none of these things would be present, if you were in charge of the world, but you're not. Hell just . . . is!

To understand why it is, we need to understand God better.

God isn't a Father Christmas, tooth-fairy, old man with a long white beard with a permanent smile and sandals, who offers nothing but love, love, love. This view is just wishful thinking.

Think how complex we are as individuals – that's why counsellors and psychiatrists are so rich! Now multiply that by an infinity or two and we're close to understanding the mind of God.

(Write GOD on chart, surrounded by the list of attributes.)

God is love – true. God is also compassionate, faithful, merciful, patient, powerful, wise, truthful . . . And God is just.

(Underline GOD is Just)

Think of your parents in this simplified example. You're good –
you get a sweetie. You're bad – you get a cuff round the ear.
There are two sides to justice.

It is because God is just that he

- Rewards some – those who accept him (indicate on chart).
- Punishes others – those who reject him (indicate on
  chart).

That's his nature.

Hell exists because there needs to be a place for those who
reject him – a place where his presence is absent *(underline on
chart)*.

Heaven equally exists for those who accept him – a place where
his presence is total *(underline on chart)*.

Remember, God doesn't want us to go to hell. Because he's a
God of love he provides a means of escape from hell.

The choice is ours.

And the best way to deal with it is:

1. Make sure you don't go there yourself.
2. Do your best to make sure that others don't either.

It's all we can do.

Discussion

Carry on the earlier discussion, focusing on whether views have
changed since then.

(If there is a real desire now to go further then we recommend you go straight to talk 34, the start of our exhaustive eight-week explanation of the gospel of Jesus Christ, or to talk 42, which does it all in two sessions, or talk 44, which does it in one session.)

Parting shot

"Hell is truth seen too late." Thomas Hobbes, philosopher

Useful resources

http://www.77talksforteens.com/talk27.htm

28
Harry Potter: Taking Over the World?

Theme

A look at Harry Potter, asking why the occult has become so popular and mainstream, and what our response should be.

Preparation

OHP/flip chart, paper and pens for all.

Presentation

We're going to have a quiz *(give out paper and pens)*.

Five questions:

1. Who is second son of Adam in the Bible? (Answer: Abel.)
2. Who was Hannah's son? (Answer: Samuel.)
3. What mountain did Noah's Ark finally settle on? (Answer: Ararat.)
4. Which apostle took the place of Judas? (Answer: Matthias.)
5. What king came after David? (Answer: Solomon.)

Before we check your answers, let's do another five questions.

1. What school does Harry Potter go to? (Answer: Hogwarts' School of Witchcraft and Wizardry.)
2. What game features in the Harry Potter books? (Answer: Quidditch.)
3. What are non-magical people called in the Harry Potter books? (Answer: Muggles.)

4. Who is the caretaker of the school in the books? (Answer: Hagrid.)
5. Who is the main villain in the Harry Potter books? (Answer: Voldemort.)

Now hands up who got more correct answers with the **second** group of questions.

(Expect this to be so, otherwise the whole argument falls flat – but trust me!)

We are more knowledgeable about a fantasy story written for small children than we are about events in the book that Christianity tells us contains the secrets of the universe.

Discussion

Hands up those who think Harry Potter books are just good, harmless fun.

Hands up those who believe that there is some truth in the world of Harry Potter, with regard to witches, magic powers, etc.

- What do we make of Harry Potter? Good harmless fun?
- What do we make of the world views presented in the books – can we believe in magic as it is portrayed in the books?

Presentation

The Sunday Times described Harry Potter as "the boy who bewitched 100 million children".

So, is there anything to be concerned about in the world of Harry Potter?

We really need to add the following, as they share similar world views – *Buffy the Vampire Slayer*, *Sabrina the Teenage Witch*, *Charmed*, etc.

The theme throughout all of these stories can be summarised in one word: **Power**. *(Write it on chart.)*

Let's face it, there's an attraction to be able to do the following things.

- Get the better of the school bully through magical powers.
- Perform awesome tricks of magic to get popular with friends.
- Exert control over others, to make them do what you want.

It's all about **power**, and the "magic" of the Harry Potter books is that someone who has been bullied and neglected and abused can, through this power, **feel good about himself** (or herself, in the case of Buffy, Sabrina, etc).

But does this power actually exist, or is it just something you find in books and TV programmes?

There are said to be around a million witches in the USA (three million worldwide) with around 5000 websites to promote their world view.

There has to be something in it.

It shares a common outlook with a lot of newer beliefs that are appearing more and more in society.

Hands up those who have any experience of the following:

Astrology (horoscopes), ouija boards, spiritualism, yoga, transcendental meditation, crystal healing, acupuncture, homeopathy *(you can add any of your own here)*.

In most cases we have no idea why things like acupuncture and homeopathy work. They just do. They all share the following idea: **if it works, do it**. *(Write on chart.)*

Similar to the Nike slogan – Just do it!

It looks at the present and provides a quick fix. It doesn't care about the future. This pays no attention to consequences.

The Bible talks of consequences, particularly in relation to the sort of magic that you will find in the Harry Potter books and the Buffy and Sabrina TV programmes.

(Read Deuteronomy 18:9–22.)

"When you enter the land the Lord your God is giving you, do not learn to imitate the detestable ways of the nations there. Let no one be found among you who sacrifices his son or daughter in the fire, who practises divination or sorcery, interpets omens, engages in witchcraft or casts spells, or who is a medium or spiritist or who consults the dead. Anyone who does these things is detestable to the Lord, and because of these detestable practices the Lord your God will drive out those nations before you. You must be blameless before the Lord your God."

This not God being a killjoy, he is talking about **real consequences** of dabbling in things we don't understand, real problems that are going to affect our lives in real ways.

But God also tells us that he can rescue us if we have gone in a bit too deep in any of these things:

(Read Romans 8:38–39.)

"For I am convinced that neither death nor life, neither angels nor demons, neither the present nor the future, nor any powers, neither height nor depth, nor anything else in all creation, will be able to separate us from the love of God that is in Christ Jesus our Lord."

This is a **real promise** to every person who accepts Jesus into their heart. They never need to fear again, because God will never abandon them, whatever they have got into.

Discussion

You may want to discuss their experiences, though there is a chance that a spirit of fear can creep into proceedings, so be warned. Perhaps you can offer to pray with individuals if they do have fears about these issues. It will be a good idea to close this session with a generic prayer, even if it is not customary to end sessions in this way – some may be fearful without showing it and a general prayer for peace and protection will be a good witness to unbelievers.

(If there is a real desire now to go further then we recommend you go straight to talk 34, the start of our exhaustive eight-week explanation of the gospel of Jesus Christ, or to talk 42, which does it all in two sessions, or talk 44, which does it in one session.)

Parting shot

Power and faith. One protects the body, the other feeds the soul. Which is more important?

Useful resources

http://www.77talksforteens.com/talk28.htm

29
So Who Is This . . . God?

Theme

Examining God, comparing Christian views with other popular views.

Preparation

OHP/flip chart.

Presentation

Who is this God?

- Is God a he, a she, or an it?
- Is God visible, invisible or metaphysical?
- Is God personal or distant?
- Is God nice or nasty?
- Is God inside you or somewhere else?
- Does God definitely exist or is it still up for debate?

We have to ask these questions because it's such a big subject. So many religions and cults lay a sort of claim to him, that we need to narrow it all down, because there's one unavoidable fact . . .

There is only one God – or at least one "god" who is "the boss".

So the question is, when Christians, Jews, Muslims, Buddhists, Jehovah's Witnesses, Hindus, Mormons, etc. pray to God . . . **are they praying to the same God?**

And, if not, who are all these other gods? Do we have an Ancient Greek, Mount Olympus situation, with a load of gods – Zeus, Apollo, Athena – all fighting for control?

Perhaps the film world can give us some clues; after all Hollywood tends to shape our thinking on so many other things.

Discussion

Any input as to how God has been depicted in films.

Here are three examples:

- Biblical epics, such as *The Ten Commandments* with Charlton Heston – God is seen as a very male, stern, judgemental, father figure.
- *Oh God* and *Oh God 2*, comedy with George Burns playing God – God is still male, but approachable and with a sense of humour.
- *Dogma*, recent thriller starring Ben Affleck and Matt Damon – God is seen as a female (Alanis Morrisette), with gentle, caring, feminine characteristics.

If we just look at other religions, let's see what their view of God is.

(Write word "MAN" at bottom of chart.)

First, let's look at Islam.

(Write word "GOD" at top of chart. Draw line from "MAN" to "GOD" with label "submission to his will" and "ISLAM".)

God is seen as one who is far away, forever hidden and never personal. Man's destiny is to try and please God by submitting to his will, as indicated in the Q'ran, the Muslim holy book. In fact the word Islam actually means "submission".

Next, Judaism.

(Write word "GOD" in middle of chart. Draw lines from "MAN" TO "GOD" and from "GOD" to "MAN" with label "relationship and remoteness" and "JUDAISM".)

God is seen as a powerful, just ruler and as a merciful, loving deliverer. God is not merely some supreme force but is a person, one with emotions of anger, sadness, and joy. He is a person with whom one can have a relationship but at the same time he has a certain remoteness.

What about Buddhism?

(Draw circular line from "MAN" and back to "MAN" with label "own spiritual paths" and "BUDDHISM".)

There is no ultimate God in Buddhism. Those who seek enlightenment are encouraged to concentrate on their own spiritual paths rather than looking for God. Many Buddhists believe the existence of suffering and evil in the world is evidence against belief in God.

And Hinduism.

(Write word "GOD" at top of chart, with other words "god" around it. Draw line from "MAN" to "GOD" with label "impersonal, many gods" and "HINDUISM".)

There are many gods in Hinduism, though they are usually seen as manifestations of one supreme being, Brahman. This being is usually seen as a supreme impersonal being, uninvolved with life on earth.

So what about the Christian view?

(Write word "GOD" in middle of chart. Draw line from "GOD" to "MAN" with label "personal relationship" and "CHRISTIANITY".)

God may be the creator, judge and lawgiver but, above all, he is a loving, personal God, concerned in every way with his creation. With other religions, man strives for God, but with Christianity **God reaches out to man**.

And how did he show this? By sending his son to live with us. More about him next week.

Discussion

If any in the group are familiar with or have a background in any of these other religions, then perhaps they can be encouraged to talk about the view of God that was taught to them.

Parting shot

(Depending on mood of the group.)

- "How can I believe in God when just last week I got my tongue caught in the roller of an electric typewriter?" Woody Allen.
- "Maybe the atheist cannot find God for the same reason a thief cannot find a policeman." Anonymous.
- "There are two kinds of people: those who say to God, 'Thy will be done,' and those to whom God says, 'All right then, have it your way.'" C.S. Lewis.

Useful resources

http://www.77talksforteens.com/talk29.htm

30
So Who Is This . . . Jesus?

Theme

Examining the person of Jesus, comparing Christian views
with other popular views.

Preparation

OHP/flip chart, various quotes printed out for various people
to read out.

Presentation

(Write word "Jesus" on chart.)

The main man. The most talked-about person in history. This
is what someone wrote about him:

(Display on chart.)

"Here is a man who was born in an obscure village, the child of
a peasant woman. He grew up in another village. He worked in
a carpenter's shop until he was thirty, and then for three years
he was an itinerant preacher. He never owned a home. He never
wrote a book. He never held an office. He never had a family.
He never went to college. He never put his foot inside a big city.
He never travelled more than two hundred miles from the place
where he was born. He never did one of the things that usually
accompany greatness. He had no credentials but himself . . . I
am far within the mark when I say that all the armies that ever
marched, all the navies that ever were built; all the parliaments
that ever sat and all the kings that ever reigned, put together,

have not affected the life of man upon this earth as powerfully as has that one solitary life."

There are three different views you can have about Jesus:

- He was a fictitious character – he was totally made up.
- He lived but he wasn't exactly the person that Christians make him out to be.
- He was (and is) exactly who Christians say he is.

(Ask for a show of hands to see how many people fall into each of these three categories.)

So let's look at each of these in turn.

1.   He never existed. *(Write on chart.)*

It is easy to come to this conclusion if you consider that most of what we know about him is written in the four Gospels (Matthew, Mark, Luke and John), which, of course, were written by Christians!

But, believe it or not, other people write about him too. *(Get different people to read out quotes.)*

Tacitus, a Roman historian, wrote in AD 112: "Nero punished with the most exquisite tortures, the persons commonly called Christians, who were hated for their enormities. Christus, the founder of the name, was put to death by Pontius Pilate . . .'

Flavius Josephus, a Jewish historian of the second century, said: "Now there was about this time Jesus, a wise man. And his conduct was good and he was known to be virtuous. And many people from among the Jews and the other nations became his disciples."

The Jewish Talmud includes anti-Christian writings, yet does not deny Jesus' existence: "On the eve of Passover they hanged Yeshu of Nazareth and the herald went before him for 40 days saying he is going forth to be stoned in that he practised sorcery and beguiled and led astray Israel."

Well, you wouldn't expect them to be complimentary!

The last word should be the entry in *Encyclopaedia Britannica*, the major reference book in the world and not a Christian book: ". . . in ancient times even the opponents of Christianity never doubted that Jesus existed."

2.   He lived but Christians have got him wrong. *(Write on chart.)*

So what are the alternatives? Here is a list of things others have said about Jesus. *(Write on chart.)*

- A great magician (New Agers).
- A prophet (Muslims).
- A wise teacher (some Jews).
- A freedom fighter (some political Christians).
- A superstar (Andrew Lloyd Webber).
- A messenger from Venus (crazy New Agers).
- A liar and a fraud or a madman (atheists, anti-Christians).

(Ask if anyone knows of other alternative views.)

If you go through the list you find that some of the views are, in fact, correct, but **incomplete** views of the Christian Jesus.

He **was** a prophet, a miracle worker, a teacher and someone offering liberation. He was all of these and more.

He may have even had a good singing voice but he certainly wasn't an extra-terrestrial, unless you count heaven as a separate planet!

As far as being a liar, fraud or madman – they would say that!

Q: Think of a political election, whether it's for a local councillor or an American president. What tactic is often used, particularly by a weaker candidate against a stronger one?

A: Discredit him with gossip and rumour. Call him a liar, a fraud, even a madman.

It's human nature. "That which they don't understand, they seek to destroy."

3.   He is just who Christians say he is. *(Write on chart.)*

So we may sneer at those who call him a liar, fraud and a madman. But how do we know if he is who Christians say he is?

Who do Christians say he is?

As I said, they call him a miracle worker, a prophet, a teacher.

But there's more than that and the clue is in the title.

Christians and Christ come from the Greek word "Christos". It means "anointed". *(Write on chart.)*

So does the Hebrew word "Maschiach", which is translated as "Messiah". "Messiah" is Jesus' title that defines who Christians say he is: the anointed one is an individual who comes from God to save his people (and ultimately the world) from their sins and enable them to get right with God.

Of course, these are Christian concepts that you may not understand . . . yet.

The key part is **getting right with God** and that is Jesus' main mission – to bring us back to where God wants us to be . . . **as his friends**.

(Do another show of hands to see how many people fall into each of these three categories after the session.)

Discussion

Discuss the findings of the poll, if significant, and talk about the person of Jesus Christ as Christians see him.

(If there is a real desire now to go further then we recommend you go straight to talk 34, the start of our exhaustive eight-week explanation of the gospel of Jesus Christ, or to talk 42, which does it all in two sessions, or talk 44, which does it in one session.)

Presentation

And to help us gain an understanding of how it all works, there is the third member of what Christians call the Trinity – the Holy Spirit, whom we are covering next week.

Parting shot

If Jesus is who he said he was, what would he think about his name being used as a swear word?

Useful resources

http://www.77talksforteens.com/talk30.htm

31
So Who Is This . . . Holy Spirit?

Theme

Examining the person of the Holy Spirit.

Preparation

OHP/flip chart.

Presentation

(Write "GOD", "JESUS" and "HOLY SPIRIT" connected in a triangle.)

The Holy Spirit is what, for Christians, ties it all together. But what is it?

Q: Who said this? "Help me, Obi-Wan Kenobi, you're my only hope."
A: Princess Leia in *Star Wars* (the original film).
Q: Classic good versus evil – but what was the special power that held it all together?
A: "The Force".

If a character possessed "the Force" and allowed it to work in and through them, they could triumph over evil and do good for all humanity. Because of this, kids of all ages began to greet each other with . . .

(Display on chart.) "May the Force be with you."

Here are the characteristics of "the Force".

- It was impersonal, a thing rather than a person.
- It had two sides – a dark side as well as a good side.
- It was a power that could be tapped into to help you win battles.

And it couldn't be more different from what Christians call "The Holy Spirit".

One problem is in the name "The Holy Spirit". To be specific, the use of the definite article.

We don't talk of **the** God, or **the** Jesus or **the** Michael Jackson.

The word "the" causes two problems.

- Firstly it makes it less personal ("George W. Bush" is more personal than "the President").
- Secondly, and most importantly, it makes it easy for us to think of the Holy Spirit as a thing or a force rather than what **he** is . . . **a person**!

Yes, as far as Christians are concerned, The Holy Spirit, or just plain Holy Spirit, is a **person**! *(Label "Holy Spirit" on chart as "a person".)*

I won't bore you with the quotes (I'll be happy to show you them later) but, unlike "the Force" in *Star Wars*, the Holy Spirit can **be grieved** (Ephesians 4:30), has an **intelligence** (Romans 8:27) and has a **mind of his own** (1 Corinthians 12:11).

So what does he do, this invisible, ghostly being (Christians sometimes also call him "The Holy Ghost")?

He's the one, as I told you earlier, who ties it all together.

- GOD *(point to chart)* is our creator, our heavenly father, the "big boss in the sky".
- JESUS *(point to chart)* is our saviour, our friend, the "one who came to live with us".
- HOLY SPIRIT *(point to chart)* is the one who lives in our heart to help us understand the things of God and live as a follower of Jesus (i.e. a Christian).

The Holy Spirit lives in our heart, not in a touchy-feely, airy-fairy fashion, but in a very real sense.

When we become a Christian, we invite the Holy Spirit to come and live in us.

Sounds spooky? It's not. It's wonderful, and you'll be amazed at the difference it makes.

He not only does the things I said, but he also:

- Makes the Bible come alive, rather than the dead book it may seem to some.
- Helps us develop our gifts so that we can be effective in our service to God and to others.
- Helps us to pray to God.
- Guides us in our daily lives.
- Stays with us and never lets us down.

Sounds too good to be true?

He comes as a free gift – available to everyone, whoever they are and whatever they've done.

Discussion

- What is the difference between the Holy Spirit, as explained, and "other" spirits as shown in such films as *The*

Exorcist or *Ghostbusters* or involved in such practices as spiritualism?

• Prepare to talk about the consequences of allowing the Holy Spirit into your heart and becoming a Christian – the cost of being a Christian.

(This is a good point. If there is a real desire now to go further, go straight to talk 34, the start of our exhaustive eight-week explanation of the gospel of Jesus Christ, or to talk 42, which does it all in two sessions, or talk 44, which does it in one session.)

Parting shot

"Every time we say, 'I believe in the Holy Spirit,' we mean that we believe that there is a living God able and willing to enter human personality and change it." J. B. Phillips.

Useful resources

http://www.77talksforteens.com/talk31.htm

32
It's All In the Code

Theme

A brief, objective look at the Bible Codes and what they tell us about God.

Preparation

OHP/flip chart. Small doll (with small piece of paper attached under its clothing – on this paper is written the words, "God is wise and powerful! Praise him for ever and ever. He controls the times and the seasons; he makes and unmakes kings; it is he who gives wisdom and understanding. He reveals things that are deep and secret; he knows what is hidden in darkness, and he himself is surrounded by light." Daniel 2:20–22). Bowl filled with murky water, small book with mocked-up title "Those incredible, sensational, amazing Bible Codes . . .'.

Presentation

There has been a great deal of fuss about the subject of the Bible codes. Best-selling books even appeared, suggesting that, by analysing the actual words in the Bible you could predict all sorts of things, from the assassination of world leaders to an earthquake in Los Angeles in 2010! It was followed by other books.

Here is one of them. *(Show book with title showing.)*

Here is my bath water from last night. *(Show bowl.)*

Here I am throwing the book into the bath water. *(Put book into bowl.)*

Here's a baby. *(Show doll.)*

Now do we . . . throw the baby out with the bath water?

Or . . . *(Take out piece of paper from doll and read it.)*

God, if you remember, knows everything and everyone. He created the world and everything in it. He also knew everything we'd get up to, including the creation of computers in the second half of the twentieth century. And why do I say that?

In 1994, three Israelis shoved the Bible – or at least the Hebrew letters of the first five books of the Old Testament – into a computer. And what they came up with absolutely stunned them.

They discovered that the original Hebrew text of the first part of the Bible contains a complex series of codes, so complex that they could not have possibly been put there by a human writer.

And they couldn't have done this without a computer, so what they found was hidden until computers were available for them to try it.

This is what they found. *(Use chart.)*

If you took the first instance of the Hebrew letter "T" in the first verse of Genesis and counted out 49 letters (why 49? 49 is a significant number in the Bible, chiefly because it is 7 × 7, a square of a perfect number, e.g. God rested on the "seventh" day) you would get the Hebrew "O".

So what?

Well, let's go on, because the next 49 letters gives you an "R", the next 49 letters an "A" and finally, the next 49 letters brings you an "H".

The word spelt is "Torah", the very name given to this part of the Bible.

The amazing thing is that exactly the same thing happens in Exodus, the second book of the Bible!

In the third book, Leviticus, the same happens, but with the Hebrew word for "God".

In the other two books, Numbers and Deuteronomy, you get the word "Torah" again, but this time it is backwards!

Statistically we are talking of odds against these combinations happening naturally at millions to one!

So, what's it all about? Is this some kind of trick?

We are talking of Hebrew letters written thousands of years ago by Jewish scribes, transcribing the words that **God inspired them to write**. They had no computer or any knowledge that one day computers would be invented.

So, if, for whatever reason, they purposely decided to include these sequences of letters, one would ask . . . why? No one could ever discover them!

The plot thickens.

• Using a similar system researchers have found the word for "Eden" (as in "garden of . . .") coded in 16 times within the section dealing with Adam and Eve, and later in the passage, where it talks about the expulsion from the Garden of Eden, they found the word "Galut" (meaning "exile") which they also found within later passages which also had "exile" as a theme.

- Perhaps more questionably they found the names Hitler and Auschwitz within the story of Noah and the names of 64 famous rabbis, all within one portion of Genesis!

There were many, many other examples. Some are authentic, others questionable. Some Christians have done a lot of research finding the name "Jesus" throughout the Old Testament, which is interesting.

Discussion

What can we conclude from this? Is this proof for the existence of God? Or is it totally bogus?

Parting shot

"I believe that God would authenticate his own true revelation by writing his signature on the pages of his scriptures. This signature would consist of evidence, knowledge and phenomenon in the text of the Bible that no unaided human could possibly have written. In other words, the genuine scriptures should contain supernatural evidence within its text that no one apart from a divine intelligence could create." Grant Jeffery, Biblical researcher.

Useful resources

http://www.77talksforteens.com/talk32.htm

33
Mad, Bad or Rad?

Theme

A look at the three possible views of Jesus. Was he seriously deluded (mad), a liar (bad), or was he actually who he said he was – the Lord ("rad" is surfing slang for excellent, very good)?

Preparation

OHP/flip chart.

Presentation

Q: Who remembers reading *The Lion, the Witch and the Wardrobe*?
Q: Who remembers who wrote it?

C. S. Lewis was the author of the Narnia kids' novels. But he was also famous for his adult Christian books. In one of them he said this, about Jesus:

(Display on chart.) "A man who was merely a man and said the sort of things Jesus said would not be a great moral teacher. He would either be a lunatic – on a level with the man who says he is a poached egg – or else he would be the Devil of Hell. You must make your choice. Either this man was, and is, the Son of God – or else a madman or something worse."

So, he was either mad or bad or he was who he said he was . . . the Son of God.

Let's start with what he said.

Jesus said he was the **Son of God**. *(Write on top middle of chart.)*

He was either **right** or **wrong**. *(Draw two lines from "Son of God", one to "right", the other to "wrong".)*

Let's be the devil's advocate (literally) and assume he was wrong.

If he was wrong then he either knew he was wrong or he didn't know he was wrong. *(Draw two lines from "wrong", one to "knew he was wrong", the other to "didn't know he was wrong".)*

Let's assume he knew he was wrong. *(Indicate on chart.)*

This would make him out to be a liar. *(Indicate on chart.)* But a stupid one.

What did he have to gain? He had plenty of opportunity to say, "Hey, guys, I was only joking," when they led him to his crucifixion, an agonising death. Would he lie knowing that he was going to die horribly and not knowing what was coming to him after death?

(Write "dying for nothing?" on chart.)

We have to assume he wasn't a liar.

So, let's go back to our chart and now assume that he **didn't** know he was wrong. *(Indicate on chart.)*

This would make him out to be a madman. *(Indicate on chart.)*

Could a madman have given us the Lord's Prayer, the parables and moral teaching that has never been equalled in the history of mankind?

Let's get serious!

But don't just take my word for it:

Napoleon Bonaparte said, "I know men and I can tell you that Jesus Christ is not a man . . . I search in vain in history to find the similar to Jesus Christ, or anything that could approach his gospel."

(Write "could a loony produce such teaching?" on chart.)

We have to assume he wasn't a madman.

So what's left?

Let's assume he was right. *(Indicate on chart.)*

And he was the Son of God.

Then what does that mean?

I'm afraid the spotlight falls on to us.

We either **accept him** or **reject him**. *(Draw two lines from "right", one to "accept him", the other to "reject him".)*

Discussion

- Does this treatment make you think more about Jesus, or want to know more?
- Are there any flaws in these arguments – are they too simplistic?

(If there is a real desire now to go further, go straight to talk 34, the start of our exhaustive eight-week explanation of the gospel

of Jesus Christ, or to talk 42, which does it all in two sessions, or talk 44, which does it in one session.)

Parting shot

Bad, mad or rad? What do **you** think?

Useful resources

http://www.77talksforteens.com/talk33.htm

PASTURES GREEN SECTION

The Gospel

There are three presentations of the gospel here:

- Eight-session presentation (talks 34–41)
  A thorough investigation of the problem of sin, the
  solution provided by Jesus and our response to Jesus.
- Two-session presentation (talks 42–43)
  Looking at the problem of sin and the solution provided by
  Jesus.
- One-session presentation (talk 44)
  A single-session investigation of the gospel.

A gospel day

It should be possible to run the first seven talks (talks 34–40)
on a single day, with the follow-up session (talk 41) on the
following week.

The programme material would cover two to three hours and
could be staggered with breaks at convenient points. Here is a
suggested format:

10.00: Session 1 (talk 34): an overview
10.30: Short break
10.45: Session 2 (talks 35–37): mankind's problem
12.00: Lunch

13.00: Session 3 (talks 38–39): the gospel
14.00: Short time for reflection
14.15: Session 4 (talk 40): decision time
15.00: Close

Talk 41, the follow-up session, can be held the next time the group meets, perhaps a week later. Alternatively, Session 1 (talk 34) could be held a week earlier as a taster session for the day.

34
The Indescribable Gift

Theme

A 'taster' session to show what Jesus offers us, compared with what the world offers us.

Preparation

Two tables, separated by a one-metre gap. On the left-hand table is an open box, wrapped in glittery paper. It has a price tag attached, with the words, "No free lunch". Inside are small sheets of paper (described later). The right-hand table also has an open box. This is plainer on the outside, though brightly coloured on the inside. It is larger than the other box. It also has a price tag attached, marked "£0.00". Inside is one small sheet of paper (described later).

Presentation

Two boxes. Two situations.

(Pick up first box.) The first box represents you and the world that surrounds you.

Q: It glitters. Why is that?
A: Because the world is like that. It flatters to deceive. It offers us bright lights, fun, excitement and entertainment.

Let's see some examples.

(Take out small sheets of paper containing words "Money", "Power" and "Sex". Read each and encourage discussion as below.)

Discussion

1. Money

   • What would you do if you won the lottery?

But . . .

   • Does money bring happiness? (Sudden wealth can bring broken marriages and relationships.)
   • Is it good to be born rich? (How many rich kids are so bored that they turn to excesses, such as drugs, drink, etc?)

2. Power

   • Would you like to rule the world?

But . . .

   • There's a saying that power corrupts and turns you into a nasty person. Are politicians nice people in real life?

3. Sex

   • Is sex all right between consenting adults?

But . . .

   • What about unwanted pregnancies, AIDS, two-timing and the breakdown of relationships?

Presentation

So, for each of these things that the world offers us, there's a down-side. It may seem glittery and exciting, but there's often a payback.

(Read the label.) There used to be a saying, "There's no such thing as a free lunch". What this means is that there's often a catch.

- Too much money – and life can just lose its challenge, with everything on a plate, leading to boredom, leading to drugs, alcohol, over-eating . . . and an early grave!
- Too much power can leave you a very lonely person, surrounded by people who fear you, but not many who truly love you.
- Sex outside a stable relationship can bring much grief, as *Eastenders* and *Coronation Street* can tell you.

(Pick up second box.) No glitter here. Seems drab on the outside (perhaps there are no rash promises), but looks a lot better on the inside. *(Take out sheet of paper.)*

Not too many things offered here. Just one, in fact.

"I have come that they may have life, and have it to the full."

Q: And who is offering this full life?
A: Jesus Christ.
Q: So what does this box represent?
A: It represents possibilities. A new life offered to all who choose to follow Jesus Christ.

It's all about one man, **not** a religious system, **not** a list of do's and don'ts. One man – Jesus.

Here is what a writer, C. S. Lewis, had to say about him.

"What are we to make of Christ?" There is no question of what we can make of Him, it is entirely a matter of what He intends to make of us. You must accept or reject the story.

The things He says are very different from what any other teacher has said. Others say, "This is the truth about the Universe. This is the way you ought to go," but He says, "I am the Truth, and the Way, and the Life." He says, "No man can reach absolute reality, except through Me. Try to retain your own life and you will be inevitably ruined. Give yourself away and you will be saved." He says, "If you are ashamed of Me, if, when you hear this call, you turn the other way, I also will look the other way when I come again as God without disguise. If anything whatever is keeping you from God and from Me, whatever it is, throw it away. If it is your eye, pull it out. If it is your hand, cut if off. If you put yourself first you will be last. Come to Me everyone who is carrying a heavy load, I will set that right. Your sins, all of them, are wiped out, I can do that. I am Re-birth, I am Life. Eat Me, drink Me, I am your Food. And finally, do not be afraid. I have overcome the whole Universe." That is the issue.

This is the man at the heart of all who call themselves Christians. He is the one who has come not just to offer us eternal life – life **after** death – but a full and meaningful life before death.

Oh, and one other thing. *(Look at price tag.)* This is how much it is going to cost you – £0.00. It's a free gift.

You want to know more?

Stick around over the next few weeks and this box . . . could be **your** box.

Follow up

As an inspiration for yourself or to reinforce the esteem in which Jesus is held by Christians it is worth listening to the awesome audio message, "Indescribable", by S. M. Lockridge, available as a link from our web page below.

Useful resources

http://www.77talksforteens.com/talk34.htm

The quotation from C. S. Lewis is from *God in the Dock* (Fount).

35
God, Unplugged

Theme

To gain an understanding of some basic attributes of God, focusing on his holiness and his love for us.

Preparation

The same two tables and boxes. The left-hand box should be closed and the right-hand box should be open. A length of string is attached to the left-hand box. A scarf, large enough to cover a face.

Presentation

So we have two boxes, one representing our lives now, in the world *(point to it)* and all it offers, and the other representing where we could be, with Jesus Christ *(point to it)* and all he offers: "I have come that they may have life, and have it to the full."

Today I am going to introduce to you the boss, the main man, the guv'nor.

Who wants to "play God"? *(Pick a volunteer.)*

Now, everyone, don't look at him. *(Place scarf over whole face and stand him facing the audience.)*

Q: Why can't we look at him?
A: Otherwise we would die!

(Read Exodus 33:20, God speaking to Moses.) "You cannot see my face, for no one may see me and live."

Q: Why do you think that is?
A: Because he is holy.
Q: Holy? What exactly does that mean?
A: Separate. Not like you and me. Pure. Perfect.

- It's like watching a player from the reserves of a lowly English third-division football team playing alongside the superstars of Real Madrid . . .
- It's like a pub singer sharing the stage with Bono of U2 . . .

. . . multiplied by about a million!

Some things just **don't** go together. It's just not in the grand scheme of things.

It's like us and God. There is something about God that separates him from us, so much so that even a man like Moses, a great friend of God, couldn't see him face to face.

It's called **holiness**.

(Tell "God" to stretch arms forwards, hands open, palms showing.)

Q: What do these open hands symbolise?
A: Openness, giving, vulnerability, humility.

God may be holy and separate from us, but that doesn't make him aloof or uncaring.

He offers us his open hands. He wishes to give us good things, to show his love for us.

Q: So, if he loves us so much, why the gap between us and this new life offered by Jesus?

To answer this you must realise that he can do exactly what he wants. He could do this . . .

("God" takes hold of the string attached to the left-hand box and swings this box into the other box.)

He could make every one of us take this free gift of "life for ever and with a purpose". But this will mean two things:

Firstly:

("God" pulls string and allows box to swing freely.)

Q: What would that make us?
A: Puppets on a string. No free will, just robots with no minds of our own. Just worker bees scampering around doing the bidding of the queen.

Love is not about control. He wants us to make our own choices, to make our own way in life, even make mistakes.

Q: So can't we just choose to accept this new and eternal life offered by Jesus?

This brings us to the **second** point:

(Move first box along desk and watch it drop into the gap.)

It can't be done.

Q: Because God is . . .
A: Holy.

This gap is all about God's holiness. We are a very long way away from God.

It means that, until we take on board a few things, we can't get to the other side and claim our reward.

But God is waiting on the other side. He wants us to cross the gap and he has a way for us to do so.

We'll find out more in the next session.

Useful resources

http://www.77talksforteens.com/talk35.htm

36
Life Is a Three-Letter Word

Theme

Introducing the concept and reality of sin, introducing the story of Adam and Eve and showing modern-day examples.

Preparation

The same two tables and boxes. The left-hand box should be open and the right-hand box should be closed. Inside the left-hand box is a selection of newspaper cuttings with representative articles dealing with the sins listed in Mark 7:20–23. Price tags are on both boxes. On the left-hand box the tag contains the word "death" and on the right-hand box the tag still says "£0.00". A large old Bible. Actors to play God, Adam, Eve and the serpent. God will again have his face covered by a scarf.

Presentation

(Pointing in turn to the boxes and the gap.) So on the left we have our life in this world, and on the right we have the promise of a new life of purpose and meaning. And in the middle, the gap that separates them.

So, why this gap?

Well it happened a long, long time ago. Let me tell you a story. *(Push both desks together. Pick up Bible, blow dust off it and read from it.)*

(Get actors to act out following scenes, while leader reads Bible verses.)

Scene one. *(Read Genesis 2:15–17.)*
So Adam, the man God had created, was told that he could do anything but eat from one particular tree. Let's see what happens next.

Scene two. *(Read Genesis 2:20b–25.)*
Eve enters into our story, a ready-made wife. They were both naked, but it didn't bother them . . . yet.

Scene three. *(Read Genesis 3:1–17a.)*
So thanks to the wiles of the serpent, the curiosity of Eve and the weakness of Adam, it all started to go wrong.

Q: What was the first thing they noticed?
A: They were naked.
Q: What did they do about it?
A: The sewed fig leaves together.
Q: So why should their nakedness bother them now?
A: Something had changed since they ate from the forbidden tree. They were no longer innocent and carefree.

Scene four. *(Read Genesis 3:8–13.)*
So everyone blamed everyone else, but the deed was done.

Scene five. *(Read Genesis 3:21–24.)*
(Move the desks apart.) They were now banished from the Garden of Eden and no longer walked with God. Something had changed in them that meant that they could no longer live in God's presence.

They had learned how to **sin**. And just as we inherit characteristics from our parents, all who followed Adam and Eve, generation after generation, inherited this ability to sin.

This sin keeps us from God and ensures that, in our natural state, we are always going to put ourselves first.

"What comes out of a man is what defiles a man. For from within, out of the heart of man, come evil thoughts, fornication, theft, murder, adultery, coveting, wickedness, deceit, licentious-ness, envy, slander, pride, foolishness. All these evil things come from within, and they defile a man." (Mark 7:20–23, RSV)

You want some proof?

Discussion

(Pass around newspaper cuttings taken from the left-hand box.) Discuss the cuttings in the light of the sins listed in Mark 7:20–23.

Presentation

(Hold up the tag on this box.)

Q: It says "death". Any idea why?
A: *(Read first part of Romans 6:23.)* "For the wages of sin is death . . ."

Sin is not good for you, then. Ultimately it leads to death. But it doesn't have to be that way. Next week we'll start looking at possible solutions to this situation.

Parting shot

Does a young child need to be taught to be bad, or does it come naturally? What does this tell you about our natural inclination?

Useful resources

http://www.77talksforteens.com/talk36.htm

37
Sticky Plasters for the Soul

Theme

Having discussed the problem of man's separation from God, we look at ways that man uses to bridge the gap, and conclude that there is nothing that man alone can do to get right with God.

Preparation

Mock microphone. Presenter in guise of roving reporter. The same two tables and boxes. The left-hand box should be open and the right-hand box should be closed. Inside the left-hand box are three long strips of paper with writing on them (see below for content). Price tags are on both boxes. On the left-hand box the tag contains the word "death" and on the right-hand box the tag still says "£0.00". Get two volunteers to play Adam and the Bible reader and give them their words to say (see below).

Presentation

PRESENTER: So here we are on planet earth and
                      this is the situation so far. Adam, the
                      first man standing and his mate, Eve,
                      have blown it big time! Paradise lost,
                      to be precise, and all because the lady
                      felt fruity and Adam couldn't let the
                      lady down. As for the snake, the last
                      we heard was that it was seen, legless,
                      in the undergrowth, eating the dust.
                      Adam and the missus were slung out
                      of the Garden to a life of trouble and

strife. And the daily chats with the
Lord God were now just history.
*(Take microphone and walk among
audience, interviewing people as
follows.)*
Adam. What's your take on this? Any
regrets?

ADAM: Well, Brian, of course if I could turn
the clock back I wouldn't have
listened to the wife, would I? Do you
think I enjoy schlepping away here in
the fields? Remember Woolly, our pet
lamb? We've just barbecued him. So
tasty! Yet an apple and an orange
would have done me when I was in the
Garden. What is happening to us?

PRESENTER: Oh, dear. Looks like your life's going
to have to change now, adapt to the
new circumstances. *(To audience.)* In
fact, everyone's life was going to
change.

BIBLE READER: *(Read Romans 5:12–14.)*

PRESENTER: This single act of disobedience by
Adam brought sin into the world, and
every man and woman in the history
of the world has suffered the
consequences. Separation from God.
The question is now, how do we get
back into God's favour? How do we
bridge the gap between man and
God? Let's ask a few people.
*(Take out the three long strips of paper
to three volunteers to read out. They
then put each strip back into the box.)*

CHARITY WORKER: I'm a fund-raiser for a foreign relief
agency. So far this year I've raised

enough cash to build a nuclear reactor for a small African village. I'm also a vegetarian and buy the *Big Issue* to support the homeless.

CHURCH MEMBER: I go to church most weeks and I help arrange the flowers. I enjoy it there because I can have a good gossip and a chat. Don't like the new vicar, though. His sermons are too long and he's a bit too religious for my liking.

GENERAL GOOD PERSON: I'm a good person. I'm kind to my old mum, my wife and my kids. I treat everyone with respect. I try hard to follow the Ten Commandments, though I don't consider myself a Christian. I live a good life and treat everyone with respect. I don't know what more I can do.

(Take the three strips of paper from the box and try to place them across the gap between the two desks. They all drop to the ground.)

PRESENTER: No sticking power!

BIBLE READER: *(Read Isaiah 64:6.)*

PRESENTER: You can be as good as you like, but it won't buy you favour with God. Think of swimming the Atlantic. Some of us can only paddle, and some of us can swim for miles and miles and miles, but it doesn't make any difference – none of us can swim well enough to get to the other side! It's all the same to God, at the end of the day – we've all failed to get to the other side and bridge the gap!

(Illustrate with the desks.)

Discussion

Encourage the group to think of people in the world who are considered "good" people, but reinforce their idea that, no matter how perfect these people seem, we all fall short of God's standards.

Presentation

So how do you get this favour with God? It reminds me of a joke. An R.E. teacher in an infant school asks the question, "What is grey, has a big bushy tail, and eats nuts?" A little kid shoots his hand up and answers, "I suppose you want me to say 'Jesus', but it sounds like a squirrel to me."

The answer is, of course, Jesus. This is a church youth group (or whatever) after all!

But you're intelligent people. Simply saying "Jesus is the answer" is not sufficient, because there also needs to be a reasonable explanation.

There's a short answer – Jesus died for my sins – which you've heard umpteen times, possibly without a good explanation. And there's a longer answer – which you're going to get next week.

Useful resources

http://www.77talksforteens.com/talk37.htm

38
No Greater Sacrifice

Theme

Having recognised that we need to be right with God, and that
we can't do it ourselves, examine God's plan for reconciliation:
the sacrificial system and the ultimate sacrifice of Jesus himself.

Preparation

The same two tables, with boxes closed.

Presentation

(Stand in gap between tables.) This was the situation. Adam
and Eve once lived in paradise, in communion with God. Then
they disobeyed the only restriction God gave them, and ate
from the tree of knowledge of good and evil. They knew evil,
they knew how to sin, and sin came into the world. People were
separated from God by the sin in their lives, their thoughts, and
their hearts. They've tried many ways to bridge the gap
between themselves and God, trying to be good, through
charity and even going to church. But it's never enough to
change their hearts.

So God set up an arrangement, a ritual to help people
understand how deep and terrible are the consequences of sin.
When people wanted to say they were sorry for their sins, and
turn over a new leaf, they sacrificed an animal. Its life was
taken, as a symbol of theirs. ("The wages of sin is death.")

(Read Leviticus 17:1.) "For the life of a creature is in the
blood, and I have given it to you to make atonement for

yourselves on the altar; it is the blood which makes atonement for one's life."

Discussion

How do we make "atonement" with our friends when we've done the wrong thing? (Flowers, kisses, apologies, chocolate.)

How long does it last? (Until the next time we're rude or thoughtless – not long usually!)

Presentation

This was OK while it worked – while people appreciated the awfulness of the sacrifice on the altar. But after a while it became just routine – they felt that they could sin as much as they liked, as long as they made the right sacrifices to God.

(Read Hosea 6:6, Proverbs 21:3.)

Q: What did God really want?
A: A change of heart, an internal change – repentance.

God had to do something, so he did. He sent his son Jesus to live among us, and to die for us. When Jesus died on the cross he showed us God's justice (the penalty for sin is still death) and his love (God himself provides the ultimate sacrifice). And by rising from the dead he showed us the glorious truth that God's love doesn't die, and that we can share in his eternal life. But although he was God, he died like any human – painfully.

(Start background music. Read Mark 15:16–37.)

We've just read what actually happened. This wasn't Hitler, Stalin, Pol Pot or Saddam Hussein who died a painful death. It wasn't any ordinary sinful man. It was the God who was present at the creation of the universe, who could have called up a legion of angels to stop it happening, who had the choice to control events. Yet he went willingly to a death he chose.

He endured:

- **mockery** – a purple robe, a crown of thorns, mock worship (Mark 15:17–18)
- **insults** – people hit him, spat on him and jeered him (Mark 15:19–20, 29)
- **pain** – the terrible pain of crucifixion.

Written records tell how the crucified person was usually stripped and laid on the ground with his arms spread out on the cross-bar. He was either tied or nailed to it, then the bar with the man hanging from it was lifted and fastened on to the vertical stake. After that, the feet were tied or nailed in place. Death came by suffocation, as the victim's chest muscles weakened, preventing breathing. To speed things up, the legs were broken so he couldn't press with his feet to enable air to reach the lungs. The pain was indescribable.

There was also the **degradation** of this death: the Jews believed that everyone who was crucified was cursed, because it was a punishment reserved for criminals.

There was something else, too. The writers of the New Testament believed that Jesus didn't just suffer physical agony on the cross, but also the penalty for the sins of the human race. *(Read Romans 8:3–4.)*

The people taunted him, saying, "Come down from the cross and we'll believe you."

He could have done so if he'd wanted. But he didn't.

Next time, we'll examine why this act of Jesus made all the difference – to this gap.

Useful resources

http://www.77talksforteens.com/talk38.htm

39
A Bridge of Tears

Theme

Exploring the core Christian belief of Jesus' death on the cross and why it provides us with salvation.

Preparation

The same two tables and boxes. Both boxes should be closed (make sure labels are still there). A volunteer to play Jesus/God (he needs to be selected earlier, so as to practise his part). A large scarf. A wooden bar (about two metres long).

Presentation

(Stand in gap between desks.) The situation so far. Because of our sin we are separated from God. Man has tried many ways to bridge this gap – through charity, good deeds or even by going to church. But none has worked, so God has provided us with a solution – the death of Jesus Christ on the cross, as we demonstrated last week.

Q: Why?
A: Firstly a sacrifice was needed so mankind could be set right with God. Secondly, the death of Jesus provided this sacrifice in a way that no previous sacrifice had ever done. In fact, no blood sacrifice was ever needed again!

But why? And how? What was so special about Jesus Christ?

Well, first, let's consider God. *(Volunteer walks over to the right-hand desk and scarf is put over his face.)*

His face is covered because of his holiness. He also loves us. So much so, that he came to live with us, as a man, as Jesus Christ, a humble Jew living 2000 years ago. *(God removes scarf from face and places it over his head, as Jewish head covering.)*

He lived among us and lived a life without sin, the Bible tells us. He healed the sick, fed the hungry, taught the people how to live good lives. But most of all, he taught people about himself, how he had come . . . to die. *(Jesus picks up long wooden bar and carries it over his shoulders, walking slowly towards gap between two desks. He then crouches so that bar rests between desks and stays there.)*

A man without sin, died for our sins.

We heard earlier that the wages of sin is death. *(Rip the tag saying "death" from the box on the left-hand side and pin it to Jesus' clothes.)*

Through our sin we deserved death, but he died instead, for everyone who had ever sinned – which means everyone who had ever lived.

We saw the physical agonies of the crucifixon, but there was more. There was the awesome spiritual burden of dying for our sins – every sin ever committed.

So he died. *(Jesus collapses on the floor.)*

But, two days later, he rose again. *(Jesus rises to his feet.)*

He had defeated death and has provided a path for us to do the same. A bridge between man and God, provided by the death and resurrection of Jesus Christ.

And he did all this for you . . . and me.

Q: What would be the situation if Jesus hadn't done what he did?

A: Everyone's sins over the past 2000 years (and possibly more) would remain "un-dealt with". Because sin separates us from God, think how far away from him you would be if Jesus hadn't provided a way to bridge this gap.

There is a way. He's provided the bridge to God, over the gap that we have found impossible to cross.

The next step is up to us, but we need to know how to travel across the bridge. Because it's a toll bridge – there's a cost involved. A personal cost. We will discover this in our next session.

Challenge

Encourage a week of prayer and contemplation of our sins, past and present. Tell people to write their sins down and seal them in an envelope. Tell them to bring the envelopes along next week. Assure them that total anonymity will be observed.

Useful resources

http://www.77talksforteens.com/talk39.htm

40
Choose Life!

Theme

Having thoroughly explained how Jesus has come to bridge the gap between man and God, we now look at what one must do in order to become a Christian.

Preparation

The two tables and boxes. The wooden bar (about two metres long) linking the two desks. The box on the right should be gift-wrapped, prepared as indicated below and closed. Some suitable tracts should be placed inside the box. The box on the left should be made of thin paper and should be open. Metal tray, matches (and some lighter fuel?). Fire extinguisher should also be to hand. Everyone should bring "sin envelopes", as suggested in the previous session.

Presentation

(Stand by the gap between desks.) To recap. Because of our sin we are separated from God. Man has tried many ways to bridge this gap – through charity, good deeds or even by going to church. But none has worked, so God has provided us with a solution – the death of Jesus Christ on the cross. The gap has been bridged by Jesus, who suffered and died in our stead, but conquered death and, by doing so, did what he said he would:

"I have come that they may have life, and have it to the full."

So let's go and claim it – after all it is a free gift. *(Show label on right-hand box, then start to move the left-hand box over wooden bar, but stop half way.)*

It may be a free gift, but we will need to know how to claim it.

Let's find out more.

(Outer wrapping of right-hand box is John 1:11–12 – the verse and its reference.)

We should now have an idea of what's on offer, a free gift to get all your sins dealt with and a restored relationship with God. Who wants it?

(Throw the box to volunteer who reads the verse.)

Jesus needs to be "received".

Q: What does this mean?
A: It's not just to believe what Jesus has done – we need to make it personal – we have to receive him into our lives, to identify with him and accept that he is our Lord and King and that we want him to be a part of us.

(Throw the same box to another volunteer who rips off the outer layer, revealing a new verse, Mark 1:15, which he/she reads.)

We need first to repent.

Q: What does this mean?
A: It simply means move away from all the bad stuff we have done and make a real effort not to repeat it.

(Ask them to put their "sin envelopes" into the left-hand box.)

These are our sins. We don't need to read them out, God has X-ray vision. But what shall we do with them – is writing them out enough? We need to **repent**, admit to God that we're willing to turn from them and put our best efforts into not repeating them.

We also need to believe.

Q: What does this mean?
A: It simply means to accept what the Bible tells us about Jesus. It requires faith.

I've given you the facts over the last few weeks. A one sentence summary is this: Do you believe that Jesus Christ, the Son of God, came into the world to die and take away your sins, providing the way for a relationship between you and God, your creator?

That's all there is to it, repent and believe.

It's easy . . . and it's hard. It's easy because **externally** it's only a matter of saying words. It's hard because **internally** it requires a complete change of heart, a willingness to admit your sins and your need for God to walk alongside you in your life.

Anyone tempted?

(Move the left-hand box to a point further across the "bridge". Throw the right-hand box to another volunteer who rips off the outer layer, revealing a new verse, Revelation 3:20, which he/she reads.)

God is waiting for you.

So, we're nearly there. Back to our sins. Anyone want to go back to their sins (joke)?

(Throw the right-hand box to another volunteer who rips off the outer layer, revealing a new verse, 1 John 1:9, which he/she reads.)

Assurance of forgiveness.

(Move the left-hand box to the right-hand desk and on to the metal tray.)

God never lies. He has given us his assurance that, because of what Jesus did on the cross, all our sins will be forgiven. So we can do this. *(Set light to sin envelopes.)*

There go your sins.

God assures us that all of these sins, however bad, can be forgiven. But not until you make the most important decision of your life.

Anyone interested in another gift, perhaps the best of all?

(Throw the right-hand box to another volunteer who rips off the outer layer, revealing a new verse, John 5:24, which he/she reads.)

The gift of eternal life.

The death of Jesus was not the end of **his** story – it was the beginning of **history**, because, just three days later, Jesus came back to life. He had cheated death – he was resurrected. He lives for ever – and so can we!

So all that and eternal life too! What a gift!

So the rest is up to you.

(Place the right-hand box back in its original place, next to the ashes of the other box.)

There is only one box left – the box with the blessings, the box with the free gift.

(Lead them through a prayer, assuring them that they don't have to make a decision now but . . . if God has been speaking to them then now's as good a time as any.)

Suggested prayer:

Lord Jesus, I admit that I have been living a life away from you and I am really sorry. I believe that you died so that I may be forgiven for all my sins. Please forgive me now. Please come into my life by your Holy Spirit and help me to live a life that would be pleasing to you. Amen.

(Open up the box. Inside will be envelopes containing the verses mentioned in today's study, or others of your choosing, or tracts for new believers. Give them out to all who want them.)

Welcome to your new life.

Parting shot

Think hard about the decision you have made and read through the scriptures and the tracts that have been given. If you need to speak to anyone, then please see me afterwards.

Useful resources

http://www.77talksforteens.com/talk40.htm

41
Life and To The Full

Theme

An open session exploring the decision made in the previous
session and discussing what should come next, introducing the
person of the Holy Spirit.

Preparation

None.

Discussion

Encourage the group to discuss whether or not they have made
decisions to follow Jesus and, if so, what God has done for
them since. Are there any testimonies? Do they have any
doubts or disappointments?

Presentation

Picture the scene. It's bonfire night. It's a bit drizzly. You have
a firework thrust into the soft earth of your back garden.
You approach it and light the fuse and stand back. It flickers
into life and then does one of two things – explodes into a
feast of sound and light . . . or fizzles out, dampened by the
rain.

It's the same when God lights your fuse!

There can be bright lights or there can be what seems to be a
damp squib.

There is no pattern. Some get the whizz bang . . . which is fine.
Others don't feel anything different . . . which is also fine.

There is one thing . . . or **person** . . . in common with both. The
Holy Spirit.

Q: The Holy Spirit? Who is that?
A: He is our new friend. He is the one we have invited into our
     lives. He is the difference between our old state and our new
     state. *(Read Romans 8:9.)*

He is **not** there to control you, to pull your strings, to take over.
You do not lose your individuality. But he will help you to
become an individual with a purpose in the new life you have
chosen. *(Read 2 Corinthians 5:17.)*

Discussion

So what happens next? What are the expectations of the group?

Presentation

Well, here are a few pointers.

Eyes. Read the instruction manual for your new life – read the
Bible.

Ears. Listen to the voice of God, in prayer, through
circumstances or through the Bible.

Legs. Leg it to a church and meet other Christians and find out
what wonderful plan God has for your life.

Arms. Roll up your sleeves and expect a fulfilling and active
life, rather than a cosy passive one.

Body. You are now part of a mystical thing called the "Body of Christ". *(Read 1 Corinthians 12:12–31.)*

Prayer

Lord, we thank you for this new life you have given us. Please lead us gently into the adventures you have for us and give us all that we need to make an impact on those around us.

Useful resources

http://www.77talksforteens.com/talk41.htm

42
Humans, We Have a Problem!

Theme

To introduce the problem of man's separation from God and what is needed for a reconciliation.

Preparation

Two tables, separated by a one metre gap. Two boxes – the left-hand box should be closed and the right-hand box should be open. A length of string is attached to the left-hand box. On the left-hand box a tag contains the word "death" and on the right-hand box a tag reads "£0.00". Inside the left-hand box is a selection of newspaper cuttings with representative articles dealing with the sins listed in Mark 7:20–23 and three long strips of paper with writing on them (see later for content). A scarf, large enough to cover a face. A large old Bible. A microphone.

Presentation

Here are two boxes. One represents our lives now, in the world *(point to the left-hand box)* and the other represents where we could be, with God *(point to right-hand box.)* And, between them, a gap – we'll find out more about that a little later.

Who wants to "play God"? *(Pick a volunteer.)*

Now, everyone, don't look at him. *(Place scarf over whole face and stand him facing the audience.)*

(Read Exodus 33:20, God speaking to Moses) "You cannot see my face, for no one may see me and live."

That is because he is **holy** – separate. Not like you and me.
Pure. Perfect.

There is something about God that separates him from us, so
much so that even a man like Moses, a great friend of God,
couldn't see him face to face.

*(Tell "God" to stretch arms forwards, hands open, palms
showing.)*

Q: What do these open hands symbolise?
A: Openness, giving, vulnerability, humility.

God may be holy and separate from us, but that doesn't make
him aloof or uncaring. He offers us his open hands – he wishes
to give us good things, to show his love for us.

So, if he loves us so much, why the gap between us and him?

To answer this you must realise that he could do exactly what
he wants. He could do this . . .

*("God" takes hold of the string attached to the first box and
swings this box into the second box.)*

He could do this.

("God" pulls string and allows box to swing freely.)

But that would make us puppets on a string. No free will, just
robots with no minds of our own. Just worker bees scampering
around doing the bidding of the queen.

Love is not about control. He wants us to make our own
choices, to make our own way in life, even make mistakes.

So why can't we just do this?

(Move first box along desk and watch it drop over the "gap".)

It can't be done. This gap is all about God's holiness. We certainly aren't holy – we're a long way away from him. And until we take on board a few things, we can't be with him. But God is waiting on the other side. He wants us to cross the gap and he has a way for us to do so.

So, why this gap?

Well, it happened a long, long time ago. Let me tell you a story. *(Push both desks together. Pick up Bible, blow dust off it and read from it.)*

Adam, the man God had created, was told that he could do anything but eat from one particular tree. Then Eve comes along, a ready-made wife. They were both naked, but it didn't bother them . . . yet.

(Read Genesis 3:1–19.) So thanks to the wiles of the serpent, the curiosity of Eve and the weakness of Adam, it all started to go wrong. Everyone blamed everyone else, but the deed was done.

(Read Genesis 3:21–24. Move the desks apart.) They were now banished from the Garden of Eden and no longer walked with God. Something had changed in them, and they could no longer live in God's presence.

They had learned how to sin. And, just as we inherit characteristics from our parents, all who followed Adam and Eve, generation after generation, inherited this ability to sin.

"What comes out of a man is what defiles a man. For from within, out of the heart of man, come evil thoughts, fornication, theft, murder, adultery, coveting, wickedness, deceit, licentiousness, envy, slander, pride, foolishness. All these evil things come from within, and they defile a man." (Mark 7:20–23, RSV)

You want some proof?

Discussion

(Pass around newspaper cuttings taken from the left-hand box.)

Discuss the cuttings in the light of the sins listed in Mark 7:20–23.

Presentation

(Hold up the tag on this box.)

Q: It says "death". Any idea why?
A: *(Read first part of Romans 6:23.)* "For the wages of sin is death . . ."

Sin is not good for you, then. Ultimately it leads to death.

PRESENTER: So here we are on planet earth and this is the situation so far. Adam, the first man standing and his mate, Eve, have blown it big time! Paradise lost, to be precise, and all because the lady felt fruity and Adam couldn't let the lady down. As for the snake, the last we heard was that it was seen, legless, in the undergrowth, eating the dust. Adam and the missus were slung out of the Garden to a life of trouble and strife. And the daily chats with the Lord God were now just history. So how do we bridge the gap between man and God? Let's ask a few people. *(Take microphone and walk among audience, interviewing people. Give the three long strips of paper to three volunteers to read out. They then put the strips back into the box.)*

CHARITY WORKER: I'm a fund-raiser for a foreign relief agency. So far this year I've raised enough cash to build a nuclear reactor for a small African village. I'm also a vegetarian and buy the *Big Issue*.

CHURCH MEMBER: I go to church most weeks and I help arrange the flowers. I enjoy it there because I can have a good gossip and a chat. Don't like the new vicar, though. His sermons are too long and he's a bit too religious for my liking.

GENERAL GOOD PERSON: I'm a good person. I'm kind to my old mum, my wife and my kids. I treat everyone with respect. I try hard to follow the Ten Commandments, though I don't consider myself a Christian. I live a good life and treat everyone with respect. I don't know what more I can do.
(Take the three strips of paper from the box and try to place them across the gap between the two desks. They all drop to the ground.)

PRESENTER: No sticking power!

BIBLE READER: *(Read Isaiah 64:6.)*

PRESENTER: You can be as good as you like, but it won't buy you favour with God.

Think of swimming the Atlantic. Some of us can only paddle, and some of us can swim for miles and miles and miles, but it doesn't make any difference – none of us can swim well enough to get there! It's all the same to God, at the end of the day – we've all failed to get to the other side and bridge the gap! *(Illustrate with the desks.)*

So how are we to do it? The answer is, of course, Jesus. But you're intelligent people. Simply saying "Jesus is the answer" is not sufficient because there also needs to be a reasonable explanation.

There's a short answer – Jesus died for my sins – which you've heard umpteen times, possibly without a good explanation. And there's a longer answer – which you're going to get next week.

Useful resources

http://www.77talksforteens.com/talk42.htm

43
Meet the Man With the Plan

Theme

Having recognised that we need to be right with God, and that
we can't do it ourselves, we examine God's plan for
reconciliation: the sacrificial system and the ultimate sacrifice
of Jesus himself.

Preparation

The same two tables, with boxes closed. The box on the right
should be gift-wrapped, prepared as indicated below. The box
on the left should be made of paper, and contain some suitable
tracts. Dramatic music. A scarf. A wooden bar (about two
metres long). A volunteer to play Jesus (he should be selected
earlier, so as to practise his part).

Presentation

(Stand in gap between tables.) This was the situation. Adam
and Eve once lived in paradise, in communion with God. Then
they disobeyed the only restriction God gave them, and ate
from the tree of knowledge of good and evil. Sin came into the
world, and man *(point to left-hand box)* and God *(point to
right-hand box)* were tragically separated. People try many
ways to bridge the gap between themselves and God, trying to
be good, through charity and even going to church. But it's
never enough to change their hearts.

So God set up an arrangement. When people wanted to say
they were sorry for their sins, and turn over a new leaf, they
sacrificed an animal. Its life was taken, as a symbol of theirs.

This was OK while it worked – while people appreciated the awfulness of the sacrifice on the altar. But after a while it became just routine – they felt that they could sin as much as they liked, as long as they made the right sacrifices to God.

(Read Hosea 6:6.)

Q: What did God really want?
A: A change of heart, an internal change – repentance.

God had to do something, so he did. He provided a special, once and for all sacrifice: his Son Jesus.

(Start background music. Read Mark 15:16–37.)

We've just read what actually happened. What was so special about Jesus?

We know about God. *(Volunteer walks over to right-hand desk.)* He came to live with us, as a man, a humble Jew. He lived a life without sin, healing the sick and teaching people how to live good lives. Most of all, he taught people that he had come to die. *(Jesus picks up long wooden bar and places it across his shoulders, walking slowly between the tables. He then crouches so that the bar rests between the tables.)*

A man without sin died for our sins – and for all the sins of everyone who had ever lived. *(Take tag saying "death" from left-hand box and pin to Jesus' clothes. Jesus collapses on to floor.)*

Two days later, he rose again. *(Jesus gets up and stands behind the bar.)* He had defeated death and provided a path for us to do the same. He'd made a bridge between us and God.

The next step is up to us, but we need to know how to travel across the bridge.

So let's go and claim the promises in this box – after all it is a free gift.

(Outer wrapping of right-hand box is John 1:11–12, the verse and its reference.)

We should now have an idea of what's on offer, a free gift to get all your sins dealt with and a restored relationship with God. Who wants it?

(Throw the box to volunteer who reads the verse.)

Jesus needs to be "received". We have to receive him into our lives, to identify with him and accept that he is our Lord and King and that we want him to be a part of us.

(Throw the right-hand box to volunteer who rips off the outer layer, revealing a new verse, Mark 1:15, which he/she reads.)

We need to **repent**, admit to God that we're willing to turn from the bad stuff and put our best efforts into not repeating it.

We also need to believe, to accept what the Bible says about Jesus.

I've given you the facts already. A one-sentence summary is this: Do you believe that Jesus Christ, the Son of God, came into this world to die and take away your sins, providing the way for a relationship between you and God, your creator?

That's all there is to it, repent and believe.

(Throw the right-hand box to volunteer who has to rip off the outer layer, revealing a new verse, Revelation 3:20, which he/she reads.)

God is waiting for you.

So, we're nearly there.

(Throw the right-hand box to another volunteer who rips off the outer layer, revealing a new verse, 1 John 1:9, which he/she reads.)

Assurance of forgiveness.

(Move the left-hand box to the right-hand table.)

Because God never lies. He has given us his assurance that, because of what Jesus did on the cross, all our sins will be forgiven.

Anyone interested in another gift, perhaps the best of all?

(Throw the right-hand box to volunteer who has to rip off the outer layer, revealing a new verse, John 5:24, which he/she reads.)

The gift of eternal life. What a gift!

So the rest is up to you.

(Place the right-hand box back in its original place. Crumple the other box and drop-kick it away.)

There is only one box left – the box with the blessings, the box with the free gift.

(Lead them through a prayer, assuring them that they don't have to make a decision now but . . . if God has been speaking to them then now's as good a time as any.)

Suggested prayer:

Lord Jesus, I admit that I have been living a life away from you and I am really sorry. I believe that you died so that I may be forgiven for all my sins. Please forgive me now. Please come into my life by your Holy Spirit and help me to live a life that would be pleasing to you. Amen.

(Open up the box. Inside will be envelopes containing the verses mentioned in today's study, or others of your choosing, or tracts for new believers. Give them out to all who want them.)

Welcome to your new life.

Useful resources

http://www.77talksforteens.com/talk43.htm

44
The Most Wonderful
Thing in the World!

Theme

To introduce the problem of man's separation from God and
how Jesus has provided the solution.

Preparation

Two tables, separated by a one metre gap. Two boxes. The left-
hand box should be open and made of paper. The right-hand
box should be closed. On the left-hand box the tag contains the
word "death" and on the right-hand box the tag reads "£0.00".
Inside the left-hand box are three long strips of paper with
writing on them (see later for content). The box on the right
should be gift-wrapped, prepared as indicated later. Some
suitable tracts should be placed inside the box. A large old
Bible. A microphone. Dramatic music (no lyrics – need to
create a mournful atmosphere). A volunteer to play Jesus (he
needs to be selected earlier, so as to practise his part). A
wooden bar (about two metres long).

Presentation

Here are two boxes. One representing our lives now, in the
world *(point to left-hand box)* and the other representing where
we could be, with God *(point to right-hand box.)* And, between
them . . . a gap.

So, why this gap?

Well, it happened a long, long time ago. Let me tell you a story. *(Push both desks together. Pick up Bible, blow dust off it and read from it.)*

Adam, the man God had created, was told that he could do anything but eat from one particular tree. Then Eve comes along, a ready-made wife. They were both naked, but it didn't bother them . . . yet.

(Read Genesis 3:1–19.) So thanks to the wiles of the serpent, the curiosity of Eve and the weakness of Adam, it all started to go wrong. Everyone blamed everyone else, but the deed was done.

(Read Genesis 3:21–24. Move the desks apart.) They were now banished from the Garden of Eden and no longer walked with God. Something had changed in them, and they could no longer live in God's presence.

They had learned how to sin. And just as we inherit characteristics from our parents, all who followed Adam and Eve, generation after generation, inherited this ability to sin.

(Hold up the tag on the left-hand box.)

Q: It says "death". Any idea why?
A: *(Read first part of Romans 6:23.)* "For the wages of sin is death . . ."

Sin is not good for you, then. Ultimately it leads to death.

So how do we bridge the gap between man and God? Let's ask a few people.

(Give the three long strips of paper to three volunteers to read out. They then put the strips back into the box. Take microphone and walk among audience, interviewing people as follows.)

CHARITY WORKER: I'm a fund-raiser for a foreign relief agency. So far this year I've raised enough cash to build a nuclear reactor for a small African village. I'm also a vegetarian and buy the *Big Issue*.

CHURCH MEMBER: I go to church most weeks and I help arrange the flowers. I enjoy it there because I can have a good gossip and a chat. Don't like the new vicar, though. His sermons are too long and he's a bit too religious for my liking.

GENERAL GOOD PERSON: I'm a good person. I'm kind to my old mum, my wife and my kids. I treat everyone with respect. I try hard to follow the Ten Commandments, though I don't consider myself a Christian. I live a good life and treat everyone with respect. I don't know what more I can do.

(Take the three strips of paper from the box and try to place them across the gap between the two desks. They all drop to the ground.)

PRESENTER: No sticking power!

BIBLE READER: *(Read Isaiah 64:6.)*

PRESENTER: You can be as good as you like, but it won't buy you favour with God.

So how do you get this favour with God? Historically, the Jews always had a way of showing God that they were sorry for their sins: they sacrificed an animal. It died instead of them, but it didn't do much to change their hearts. But now God did something amazing. He provided a sacrifice for everyone's sins: Jesus.

(Start background music. Read Mark 15:16–37.)

We've just read what actually happened.

What was so special about Jesus Christ? He lived among us and he lived a life without sin. He healed the sick, fed the hungry, taught the people how to live good lives. But most of all, he taught people about himself, how he had come . . . to die.
(Jesus picks up long wooden bar and carries it over his shoulders, walking slowly towards gap between two desks. He then crouches so that bar rests between desks and stays there.)

A man without sin, died for our sins. *(Jesus collapses on the floor.)*

But, two days later, he rose again. *(Jesus rises to his feet and stands behind bar.)*

He had defeated death and has provided a path for us to do the same. A bridge between man and God, provided by the death and resurrection of Jesus Christ.

The next step is up to us, but we need to know how to travel across the bridge.

It may be a free gift, but we still need to know how to claim it.

Let's find out more.

(Outer wrapping of right-hand box is John 1:11–12 – verse and reference. Throw the box to volunteer who reads the verse.)

Jesus needs to be "received". We have to receive him into our lives.

(Throw the box to another volunteer who rips off the outer layer, revealing a new verse, Mark 1:15, which he/she reads.)

We need first to repent. We have to move away from all the bad stuff we have done and make a real effort not to repeat it.

We also need to believe, to accept what the Bible tells us about Jesus. It requires faith.

I've given you the facts already. A one-sentence summary is this: Do you believe that Jesus Christ, the Son of God, came into this world to die and take away your sins, providing the way for a relationship between you and God, your creator?

That's all there is to it, repent and believe.

(Throw the box to another volunteer who rips off the outer layer, revealing a new verse, 1 John 1:9, which he/she reads.)

Assurance of forgiveness.

(Throw the right-hand box to volunteer who rips off the outer layer, revealing a new verse, John 5:24, which he/she reads.)

The gift of eternal life.

So the rest is up to you.

(Place the right-hand box back in its original place. Crumple the other box and drop-kick it away.)

There is only one box left – the box with the blessings, the box with the free gift.

(Lead them through a prayer, assuring them that they don't have to make a decision now but . . . if God has been speaking to them then now's as good a time as any.)

Suggested prayer:

Lord Jesus, I admit that I have been living a life away from you and I am really sorry. I believe that you died so that I may be forgiven for all my sins. Please forgive me now. Please come into my life by your Holy Spirit and help me to live a life that would be pleasing to you. Amen.

(Open up the box. Inside will be envelopes containing the verses mentioned in today's study, or others of your choosing, or tracts for new believers. Give them out to all who want them.)

Welcome to your new life.

Useful resources

http://www.77talksforteens.com/talk44.htm

MOODY BLUE SECTION

Assurances and First Steps

45
Just Little Old Me

Theme

How God sees us and cares for us and how he knows every detail about our lives.

Preparation

OHP/flip chart to illustrate points.

Presentation

Let's do a silly classroom test. Fill in the gaps:

A _____ of seagulls, a _____ of lions, a _____ of geese.
(Answers: flock, pride, gaggle.)

Q: How about this one. What do we call a large group of people?
A: A crowd, mob, the "general" public (who are the "specific" public?) etc.

Let's be more specific, because society classifies us in quite a few different ways. Let's do a test.

1: What do they call people who buy things? (consumers)
2: People who travel to work? (commuters)
3: People over 18 with privileges? (voters)
4: People who walk? (pedestrians)

And who on earth are "the public" or "the public at large"? Who are the "private", then? Those people who don't exist? Illegal immigrants?

We're also classified according to social classes. What are you? A1? B1? A2?

How impersonal. We can be grouped in so many ways. What are we – cattle?

Let's narrow it down to the individual.

(Write all the following down on chart to give an idea of different ways one individual can be known – add your own and brainstorm for others.)

- To your boss you're Mr (surname).
- To your friend you're John, smelly, shorty, the geezer.
- To phone shopping organisations we're just a postcode and a credit card number.
- To on-line shopping sites we're an e-mail address (and a credit card number).
- To government agencies we're a social security or national insurance number.

I'm not a number! I'm a free man! (This is a reference to the cult 1960s sci-fi TV, *The Prisoner*.)

You can see their point. Each of us can be uniquely defined by numbers. It helps us to be tracked and identified.

After all, it's easier and more accurate to think of you as YY 19270PD 56TY (there's only one of these) than John Smith (there are thousands of these).

Not so with God.

He knows you by your name. He doesn't need a unique number for you in case he confuses John Smith of Park Road, Epping with John Smith of Park Way, Epping – he knows him personally, too!

Talking to the prophet Jeremiah, he tells him: "Before I formed you in the womb I knew you . . ." (Jeremiah 1:5).

He knew all about us even before we were born!

In Psalm 139: 16, we read "All the days ordained for me were written in your book before one of them came to be."

And this is true for everyone – whether Christian or non-Christian. Every one of us – individually – is known by God.

He knows who you are. He's a personal God, not a God, as is thought by some, who kick-started the universe and let us all get on with it!

He cares about each and every one of us.

Matthew 10:30 says "and even the very hairs of your head are numbered". He knows and cares about every aspect of our lives.

He also knows what you've done!

And this matters. Let's read what is promised at the very end of time (Revelation 20:11–15). *(Display on chart.)*

"Then I saw a great white throne and him who was seated on it. Earth and sky fled from his presence, and there was no place for them. And I saw the dead, great and small, standing before the throne, and books were opened. Another book was opened, which is the book of life. The dead were judged according to what they had done as recorded in the books. The sea gave up the dead that were in it, and death and Hades gave up the dead that were in them, and each person was judged according to what he had done. Then death and Hades were thrown into the lake of fire. The lake of fire is the second death. If anyone's name was not found written in the book of life, he was thrown into the lake of fire."

He knows what you've done.

And how do you get into this book of life? Don't worry, because if you're a Christian, you're in it. The book contains the names of all the future citizens of heaven.

Is your name in the book of life?

Discussion

How can you be sure that your own name is in the book of life? (Offer them the assurances of salvation, i.e. not to doubt their salvation or whether they are written in the book of life: 1 John 5: 11–12.)

Useful resources

http://www.77talksforteens.com/talk45.htm

46
Who Am I Now?

Theme

When we become a Christian we become a new creation, but we also receive a lot more, in terms of identity and promises. This talk explores this situation.

Preparation

OHP/flip chart to illustrate points. Bibles for all. A handout listing today's verses. Salt cellar, candle and matches, completed jigsaw or airfix model, labels, pictures of child, vine, Jesus, army recruitment, alien.

There may not be enough time to cover all of the points made here, in which case select those you feel more comfortable with.

Presentation

So you've taken the plunge and become a Christian and God has commissioned me to present you with your welcoming letter. And here it is. *(Wave a letter.)* He's also provided a few visual aids to drive the points home. *(Read from the letter.)*

Dear Friends

We thank you for your decision to join our most exclusive club. We ask for no subscriptions and there are no hidden extras. But we challenge you to find a better list of benefits. So, let's have a look at some of your inheritances as a "born again" Christian.

(As objects and pictures are shown, keep them in view and stick labels on them with the titles.)

(Show salt cellar and lit candle and encourage them to guess the title then read the verse.)

- I am the **salt of the earth** (Matthew 5:13).
- I am the **light of the world** (Matthew 5:14).
- I am a **son of light** and not of darkness (1 Thessalonians 5:4–5).

Discussion

In the light of these verses, how should we be conducting ourselves as Christians in the world?

Presentation

(Show picture of child and encourage them to guess the title then read the verse.)

- I am a **child of God** (John 1:12).
- And I will **resemble Christ** when he returns (1 John 3:1–2).

Discussion

Bearing in mind that we have joined a new family, what are our responsibilities to our new father?

Presentation

(Show picture of a vine and encourage them to guess the title then read the verse.)

- I am part of the **true vine**, a channel of Christ's life (John 15:1–5).

Discussion

As part of this true vine what must we do to remain in it?

Presentation

(Show depiction of Jesus and encourage them to guess the title then read the verse.)

- I am **Christ's friend**, chosen and appointed by Christ to bear his fruit (John 15:14–16).

Discussion

Now that you have a new friend, what do you need to do to develop this new relationship?

Presentation

(Show completed jigsaw, airfix model, etc. and encourage them to guess the title then read the verse.)

- I am a **new creation** (2 Corinthians 5:17).
- I am **God's workmanship**, his handiwork, born anew in Christ to do his work (Ephesians 2:10).

Discussion

What must we do to make sure that our old ways don't hold us back in our new life?

Presentation

(Show picture of army recruitment poster or similar and encourage them to guess the title then read the verse.)

- I am **chosen of God**, holy and dearly loved (Colossians 3:12–14).

Discussion

As a chosen person, what should your attitude be to the other chosen people?

Presentation

(Show picture of E.T. or a Martian or similar and encourage them to guess the title then read the verse.)

- I am an **alien and a stranger** in this world in which I temporarily live (1 Peter 2:11–12).

Discussion

How then are we expected to live our lives in the world?

Challenge

(Give out handouts with all these verses and titles.)

Read through these promises and try to memorise any of them that you find particularly significant.

Useful resources

http://www.77talksforteens.com/talk46.htm

47
All Together Now

Theme

Investigating Christians as the body of Christ, rather than just
a collection of individuals.

Preparation

OHP/flip chart. A small knitted garment, e.g. a patch, square,
scarf. Another similar garment, but in a more bedraggled state,
i.e. full of holes. Some strands of wool (about one foot each) –
the same number as there are people in the audience – perhaps
tie an individual name tag to each. A shorter strand with
leader's name attached.

Presentation

Here you all are – all individuals. *(Hold strands up one by one.)*

And here's mine – mine's shorter as I'm more humble than you.
(Hold leader's strand.)

But you are also Christians, which means we're not just
individuals.

(Read Romans 12:5.)

(Display on chart.) ". . . so in Christ we who are many form
one body, and each member belongs to all the others."

(Hold strands in fist, allowing them to hang free.) So we're all
joined together.

(Tie a knot at the top.) One body, with Christ at the head.

Is this a good picture of how it works? All joined individually to Christ, but hanging free, free to exercise our individuality. It's all a bit loose, a bit flimsy. *(With other hand push fist through the strands.)*

No resistance, no real unity.

Perhaps this is a better picture. *(Show knitted garment.)*

Here all the strands are knitted together to form something a bit more substantial. *(With other hand push fist into garment, which stops fist from passing through it.)*

Let's read the next few verses in Romans.

(Read Romans 12:6–8.)

So we all make up this garment, this body of Christ, but we all have a different role. We're all called in **different** ways.

• Some of us have very definite gifts before we become a Christian, that God will develop and use in his service.

How many of you feel that this is you? *(Encourage discussion if they wish to talk about it.)*

• Others are given new gifts by God after they become believers, which is exciting – though you may have to be patient.

How many of you feel that this is you? *(Encourage discussion if they wish to talk about it, emphasising that God gives us all gifts, but it may take us time to discover them.)*

As Christians we are all called to work **together.**

If we don't . . . this could happen! *(Show bedraggled knitted garment.)*

Some are using their gifts together, but others are still acting as individuals. *(With other hand push fist into garment, which stops fist, but one or two fingers stick out through holes.)*

We are a **community of God's people**, and that's just another name for "Church".

And, for the community rules, let's read the rest of this chapter of Romans.

(Read Romans 12:9–21.)

Discussion

Discuss the practical details of these verses. How difficult or easy are these injunctions? Which are the most challenging? (Perhaps just concentrate on one or two of these verses.)

Useful resources

http://www.77talksforteens.com/talk47.htm

48
All This and a Hot-line Too!

Theme

An introduction to prayer and assurances of answered prayer.

Preparation

OHP/flip chart to illustrate points.

Presentation

Here's a little quiz. *(Keep giving clues until they get it.)*

- What happened on 14 April 1912?
- In mid-Atlantic?
- To Leonardo DiCaprio and Kate Winslet?

The sinking of the *Titanic*.

You're the wireless operator on board and you're furiously tapping out your S.O.S. in Morse code. The ship is sinking and you desperately need help.

Q: What happened next?
A: Help came too late and 1500 people drowned (700 were saved).

In fact, a nearby ship could have rescued many of them, but its radio operator was fast asleep!

Think how things could have been if the radio operator on the *Titanic* had had the **assurance** that his call had been answered and help was on its way.

Think how many happy kids there would be if their letters to Father Christmas were answered!

Think how many relieved men there'd be if their "just saying sorry" flowers had the desired effect!

Life just doesn't give you these assurances.

But God **does**!

(Read John 16:24.)

Discussion

So what prayers are answered?

Clue: How many Christians do you know with flashy sports cars, mansions, luxury yachts? *(If they do, then suggest that they are not likely to be the result of prayer!)*

Presentation

What is your image of prayer?

(Indicate the following on chart and get them to choose the right one.)

- A group of people in a circle getting embarrassed.
- A noisy gathering with many strange tongues and hallelujahs.
- A minister reading from an old book at the front of a church.

- England game just before a David Beckham free kick.
- A two-way chat between a person and God.

(All (except the fourth!) are valid images, though the last one is the preferred one.)

(Write the words "GOD" (large) and "man" (small) as an illustration to the following.)

Here's God – the creator of the universe and the sustainer of our lives. *(Indicate.)*

Here's you – one of many billions of God's creations. *(Indicate.)*

(Draw a dotted line between the two, with two arrows pointing in both directions.)

- A hot-line between the two – open at all times and you can even reverse the charges (he's already paid the price!).
- The communication is two way – you talk, he listens – he talks, you **try** to listen.

So what do you talk about?

(Read Philippians 4:6.)

Ask him anything, just like speaking to your best friend. He's your **real** best friend, if you only knew it, and he's available 24/7, wherever you find yourself. And, unlike your earthly friends, he's not going to "throw a moody" at you or only half-listen, and he's never going to say "can you stop going on about this – you're driving me mad!"

Let's read again. Jesus was speaking to his disciples shortly before his death. *(Read John 16:24.)*

Q: What's the main difference between this action and, say, writing a letter to Father Christmas?
A: You are asking in the name of Jesus.
Q: What's the significance of this?
A: By asking for something in his name, you are asking **in his authority**, because, as a Christian, you now belong to him.

Just like if you join a club, user group, fan club or whatever, there are privileges of membership, so you are given the ultimate privilege in that, whatever you ask God in prayer, he's not going to pretend he can't hear you. He will always listen.

Next week we'll cover exactly what we should be praying about.

Discussion

So enough theory, already. Let's exercise our prayer muscles.

Discuss how this particular group can pray together. Perhaps it is not mature or bold enough for corporate prayer. If not, then how about allocating five minutes or so for private prayers.

Challenge

Keep a prayer diary until next meeting and be prepared to talk about any answered prayer at the next meeting – though this should not be a compulsory option, otherwise some may not turn up out of fear or perceived failure. Mention that God's timetable doesn't always fit in with any timetables we may set, so it's not a failure if he doesn't answer your prayers when you expect him to!

Useful resources

http://www.77talksforteens.com/talk48.htm

49
Having a C.H.A.T. With God

Theme

More about prayer – practical aspects.

Preparation

OHP/flip chart to illustrate points. Bibles for all.

Presentation

Last time we discovered that prayer is "having a chat with God". *(Write "CHAT with God" on chart, with CHAT written vertically.)*

And, guess what, we're looking at a mnemonic here. But an easy one, and an obvious one, and why hasn't anyone discovered it before? We'll take them one at a time.

C – Confess your sins. *(Write on chart.)*

Why first? And why so important? Have you ever:

- Used a toilet with a blocked up "U" bend?
- Watered plants with a knotted-up hose?
- Eaten a curry after a large Big Mac meal?

The key word here is **blockage**.

Think of confession as spiritual laxative (if you'll excuse the image!).

How can we do the other stuff in our prayers if we haven't cleared out all the dung first?

And what do we need to get rid of? **Unconfessed sin**, that's what!

(Read 1 John 1:9.)

So we need to purify ourselves from all the rubbish that is blocking our communication and relationship with God.

Think about times you were angry, unforgiving, greedy, violent, ungrateful – we'll leave it for you to fill in the gaps.

So, confession is . . . saying sorry to God for all that stuff **and meaning it!**

You do that first and, as he says, he'll forgive you and allow you to get on with your life and . . . the next stage.

H – Hallelujah! *(Write on chart.)*

Hallelujah – a Hebrew word meaning (believe it or not) – Praise the Lord!

Some churches throw these around like they're going out of business, others speak them through clenched teeth and knotted tongues.

Frankly, God doesn't mind . . . as long as you really mean it and are not on a "hey, look at me, I'm a holy person" trip.

You may ask why God needs them but it's more important to turn it around and look at why we need to give them. It's called being grateful . . . to the nth degree.

Hey, as a Christian – with the promise of eternal life and an ever-present helper in this one – you've got a lot to be grateful for!

But there's more.

Praise is **uplifting** – let's read together Psalm 8. (*Or Psalm 30, or any suitable Psalm for your group.*)

So, praise is an important part of your prayer life. If words don't come easily to you, try memorising snatches from Psalms or the chorus from relevant worship songs.

Hallelujah!

Discussion

Discuss Psalms and worship songs that have meaning for people. Get some personal testimonies.

Presentation

A – Ask! *(Write on chart.)*

Let's face it, this is the part of prayer that comes most naturally to us. We'd like it to be the first part and it should really go at the end – but what sort of mnemonic is **CHTA**?

(Read John 16:24.)

We read this last time. "Ask and you will receive."

Well, just let it rip! You've got his attention – now's your big chance!

● Ask for . . . a sports car . . . and receive!

- Ask for . . . the latest computer console . . . and receive!
- Ask for . . . buckets of cash . . . and receive!

After all, he's got to deliver . . . he's promised. **Hasn't he**?

You've got to be joking!

Remember, you're praying in Jesus' name, as a Christian, so do you **really** think it's relevant to pray for a car, a computer, lots of cash?

Do you think Jesus accepted you into his kingdom just for you to get rich and collect lots of possessions?

Or perhaps he chose you to join him because he's got a job for you to do on earth.

- If you join Madonna's fan club, you're not going to get discounts on Kylie Minogue posters!
- If you joined the Microsoft Windows user group there's no point plaguing them with questions about double glazing!

No, you've joined a very special organisation – a worldwide network of like-minded individuals dedicated to Jesus Christ and helping others to find peace with God.

With that in mind, you pray accordingly. No selfish prayers, just prayers from the heart of a Christian.

Discussion

Discuss the sort of things that are valid petitions.

Presentation

T – Thanks. (*Write on chart.*)

Last but **not** least!

Surely, you've got lots to thank him for. For a start, the fact that he accepted you in the first place!

But, as you mature as a Christian, you'll realise that prayers you've prayed before have been answered – perhaps not in the time frame you requested, or in the way that you wanted, or even with the decision you expected.

We will cover these issues next week.

But let us finish with another Psalm, which we'll read together.

(Read Psalm 63:1–8.)

Discussion

So enough theory, already. Let's exercise our prayer muscles.

Use C.H.A.T.

Discuss how this particular group can pray together. Perhaps it is not mature or bold enough for corporate prayer. If not, then how about allocating five minutes or so for private prayer?

Useful resources

http://www.77talksforteens.com/talk49.htm

50
So Where Do We Go From Here, Lord?

Theme

What happens after we pray?

Preparation

OHP/flip chart to illustrate points. Bibles for all. Small ball.

Presentation

(Write "CHAT with God" on chart, with CHAT written vertically and words "confess", "hallelujah", "ask" and "thank" highlighted.)

So we offer our prayers to God. We confess, we Hallelujah and we thank him – and all these are different from the other one – the **asking** bit. The first three we leave with him, because they are for him. But the last one, where we are asking God for whatever . . . we expect him to act.

Q: Anyone heard of Cartesian logic?
A: Where there's a cause there's an effect.

(Throw a ball at someone.)

I throw the ball – that is the cause
You catch it – that's the effect.

I ask God for something – that is the cause
He answers it – that is the effect.

But it's not that straightforward.

Think how difficult it must be for him. He must get, what, one,
two million prayer requests a day? These have all got to be
sorted and classified by the incoming angels, fed through the
network to God who has to multitask like nobody's business.
Once processed, each prayer answer has to be sorted by time
and place to the relevant outgoing angels, who have to whisk
them back to the right person. Occasionally mistakes are made,
of course, what do you expect? Someone will occasionally grow
an extra leg, a retired man from Cleethorpes may get the OK to
marry that student he's never heard of. It happens!

No, it doesn't!

That's how it would work if we were in charge, and how it
possibly does work in Lapland – how often does Father
Christmas send out the wrong present?!

(Read Matthew 21:22.)

It **seems** straightforward. But the mechanism is simple and for
that we go back to our cause and effect.

You see there is always an effect. God **always** answers prayer.

He may say one of three things. (*Write on chart.*)

- Yes
- No
- You'll have to wait!

There are many factors involved.

Discussion

What reasons can there be for not getting a "Yes", or a positive outcome, from God? *(List them on the chart – look for sin, doubt, God's sovereign choice, conscience, not having a good heart about it. Suggest reading the following scriptures and discuss.)*

- Psalm 66:18 (sin)
- James 1:6–7 (doubt)
- Hebrews 11:6 (faith)
- Psalm 24:3–4 (clean heart)
- Matthew 6:6–7 (heartfelt)

Go over personal testimonies and examples of answered prayer, perhaps you the presenter have some good testimonies, personal or otherwise.

Presentation

Hudson Taylor, the missionary to China, said, "Prayer power has never been tried to its full capacity. If we want to see Divine power wrought in the place of weakness, failure, and disappointment, let us answer God's standing challenge, 'Call unto me, and I will answer thee, and show thee great and mighty things of which thou knowest not'."

Prayer is an awesome thing. But we need to do it the right way.

(Read Philippians 4:4–7.)

Discussion/Prayer

So enough theory, already. Let's exercise our prayer muscles.

Use C.H.A.T.

Discuss how this particular group can pray together. Perhaps it is not mature or bold enough for corporate prayer. If not, then how about allocating five minutes or so for private prayer.

Useful resources

http://www.77talksforteens.com/talk50.htm

51
What Would Jesus Do?

Theme

To be challenged by the WWJD movement, inspired by the
book *In His Steps*, and considering the question, "What would
Jesus do?" in any situation.

Preparation

OHP/flip chart. A copy of *In His Steps* by Charles Sheldon, a
WWJD bracelet (or you can buy enough to give out to the
group).

Presentation

So you're a Christian now? Well done, give yourselves a clap.

What now? Do we just sit around and wait for heaven? Or is
there something else we should be doing?

Discussion

What should we be doing next, once we become Christians?

Presentation

We should seek to be **more and more like Jesus**.

(Read Romans 8:16–17.)

OK, so we're not sinless and perfect like him, so he sets a
difficult target. It doesn't mean that we shouldn't give it a try.

- Tell that to Accrington Stanley in the F.A. Cup.
- Tell that to your granny as she trains for the London Marathon.
- Tell that to the Liberal Democrats.

They don't expect to win, but they're willing to take part and give it their best shot!

But, as Christians, perhaps we have a better incentive and some have taken it very seriously.

A book was written over a hundred years ago, called *In His Steps*. It is one of the most read Christian books of all time and is said to have changed many lives around the world.

It is a work of fiction and it poses one simple question.

"What would Jesus do?" *(Write on chart.)*

The heroes of the book were challenged to live one year of their lives not making any major decision without considering this question.

It seems simple because, after all, as Christians, aren't we meant to do this **anyway**?

But in the book we see the sacrifices that had to be made, the ridicule the people attracted, and their loss of social standing and respect. But they emerged victorious, after many battles.

A few years ago, in Michigan, USA, a Christian youth group took up the challenge and started up a new movement called WWJD – What would Jesus do?

(Show WWJD bracelet and give them out if you have them.)

Around 14 million of these have been sold worldwide. A good witness . . . and good business!

The idea is that the bracelet should remind you to think "What would Jesus do?" in any situation you find yourself in.

A youth leader in the USA compiled the following list of possible actions, where you should consider the WWJD message before deciding what to do. *(Display on chart.)*

- Hang out with people who treat others badly.
- Hug a stranger who has AIDS.
- Cheat on a test to get a passing grade.
- Help a relative die who has a terminal illness.
- Stay at a party where people are drinking.
- Copy answers from a friend's homework.
- Keep the money when the cashier gives you too much change.
- Smoke a cigarette.
- Lie to your parents.
- Rush to make it to school on time.
- Maintain sexual purity.
- Spread rumours about someone who hurt you.
- Lie for a friend to a person in authority.
- Be the first to talk to the new person in school.
- Date someone who doesn't believe in God.
- Sneak out after curfew.

Discussion

Think about the practical implications (perhaps use the above list). Go over decisions people in the group have made recently and whether they made these decisions in the light of WWJD.

Challenge

For the next week wear the bracelets and, if possible, read the *In His Steps* book. Tell them to remember all main decisions they make that week and to be ready to talk about them the following week.

The next week, if the WWJD exercise has challenged them, think about joining the worldwide WWJD movement, or at least keeping the experiment going for the foreseeable future.

Useful resources

http://www.77talksforteens.com/talk51.htm
In His Steps by Charles Sheldon (Zondervan).

52
Reading the User's Manual. Part 1

Theme

Learning to take the Bible seriously and developing a desire
and a strategy to stick to some sort of reading plan.

Preparation

OHP/flip chart. Bibles for all.

Presentation

A number of scenarios: there's a rattling under the bonnet of
your car, your PC's CD-ROM drive is not working, your TV is
not picking up Channel 4 (a blessing in disguise!).

Q: What do you do – assuming you're the sort of person that
likes to sort things out yourself?
A: Consult the user's manual.

More scenarios:

• You're a Christian now, but your girlfriend isn't, what do
you do?
• Your best friend is pregnant and wants an abortion, what
can you say?
• You like the odd drop of beer, but lately you've been
drinking a bit too much – is this wrong?

Q: What do you do – assuming you're the sort of person that
wants to sort things out?
A: Consult the user's manual – the Bible.

(Hold up the Bible.)

Easier said than done? Have you seen the size of this book?
And where's the index?

The Bible is a magical book, not a book of magic. It is a
timeless classic, full of human stories that address the problems
of mankind in the twenty-first century. We have enough lust,
envy, jealousy and pride in the Bible to excite any soap fan. The
Bible has the love stories and the triumphs against all the odds
to warm the hearts of the most romantic fiction devotees. And
there's sufficient blood, violence and retribution to excite the
passions of . . . well, there's a bit of blood and, although it's
not always in the best possible taste, it's there for a reason.
That's the point of the Bible. Everything is there for a reason,
because there is **one** author, God himself, and he sure knows
how to write a book!

OK. But how can we really use this book?

I'm a Christian and really want to get into God's word, to learn
more about him and find out how I should live, but this is all a
bit daunting. Where do I start?

- Chronologically (read from Genesis 1:1)?
- Randomly – without prayer (open book at random and
  read a line)?
- Randomly – with prayer (close eyes and look pious, then
  open at random and read a line)?
- Or do you have a plan (cunning or otherwise)?

Discussion

Any suggestions? How do the group read the Bible at present?
List their methods and discuss the pros and cons of each
from your experience, perhaps bringing in some of the

monthly Bible reading guides, particularly those relevant to teenagers.

Presentation

So we've talked about plans for reading the Bible. But these are not going to do anything for you if your attitude is not right.

(Write following on chart.)

1. Realise that, however you read this book, it is going to be **God's main way of speaking** to you, both in teaching you more about himself, or through giving you specific help in any situation. He will often answer prayers by directing you to a given verse in the Bible.
2. Make sure then that you do stick to any plan you have for reading the Bible, whatever it is – even if it's just for five minutes a day (or less). He can't speak to you if you ain't listening!
3. Before you pick up the book, pray for **the Holy Spirit** to help you to understand or see the significance in what you are about to read. Otherwise it's like playing an electric guitar without the electricity! The Holy Spirit is the difference between the Bible being just a good book of stories or your own personal user manual.

You've heard many famous Bible stories before – David and Goliath, Noah and the flood, Abraham and Isaac, etc., but, when you read them for yourself with the right attitude . . . they will come alive. God will show you new things you haven't seen before.

Try reading it for yourself.

Challenge

What do you know about the book of Jonah? Next week we are going to find out a lot more and I encourage you to give it a read first – there are only four chapters in it.

Useful resources

http://www.77talksforteens.com/talk52.htm

53
Reading the User's Manual. Part 2

Theme

Reading through the first part of the book of Jonah and considering such topics as personal evangelism and God's calling.

Preparation

OHP/flip chart. Bibles for all.

Discussion

Ask them to list anything they have learned, or key points, from reading the book of Jonah (if they did actually read it).

(Note them down on chart.)

Presentation

So, for those of you who took the trouble to read it, there was some stuff there that you didn't expect. The Bible is like that – you can read parts of it again and again and you will often discover something new each time.

Jonah's job. *(Read Jonah 1:1–2.)*

Jonah wasn't an ordinary Joe – he was a prophet of God, and in fact already appears elsewhere in the Bible (in 2 Kings 14:25).

Q: Where was Nineveh and what was the significance of it?
A: Nineveh was the capital city of the largest empire of the time and the biggest threat to Jonah's people, the Jews. It was also a very wicked place.

Jonah's reaction. *(Read Jonah 1:3.)*

Q: Why did he run away?
A: The answer is in Jonah 4:2. He set himself up as judge and jury and felt that the people of Nineveh were too wicked to be saved and that God was being too merciful to them! In short, he hated them too much!

Discussion

How do we feel about trying to reach people who we feel don't deserve salvation? Should God have accepted deathbed confessions from Hitler, Stalin (or any other godless tyrant you can think of)?

Q: Who deserves salvation?
A: In fact no one **deserves** it, but God offers it to everyone anyway, however bad their behaviour, from school bullies to serial killers.

The parable of the unmerciful servant. (*Read Matthew 18:23–35.*)

This man owed over a million pounds and had this debt cleared, but he refused to do the same to someone who owed him only a few pounds! He was found out, and because of his lack of forgiveness had to cough up the million pounds or so, after all!

Remember, this is a **parable** – it's teaching us general principles. The principle here is to treat others how we have been treated ourselves, by God.

When we become Christians, God forgives us of all our debts (we call them sins), but if we're going to begrudge this gift to those we don't like, then we don't deserve our own salvation!

So we must be ready to speak our faith to everyone, to the unlovely as well as the lovely, to enemies as well as friends.

They all deserve it equally – no one is more deserving of eternal life than anyone else.

That's how it works. We don't make the rules. Before we became believers, perhaps we were unlovely, or someone's enemy.

Challenge

Speak to someone unlovely with love over the next week.

Presentation

Jonah's fate. *(Read Jonah 1:4–17.)*

So he ran off in the exact opposite direction – he was making a point! Did he really think that God couldn't find him? Well, God found him and made sure that everyone knew it!

He could have just had him dumped at sea – but he had him rescued in a most unlikely way – in the belly of a whale (or large fish).

Discussion

Has anyone tried to run away from God? Any testimonies? Has God called anyone here to a task that they didn't feel up to doing? If so, do they want to talk about it? God does not make mistakes, but sometimes we have to work things through.

Presentation

Jonah's prayer. *(Read Jonah 2.)*

Jonah realised that, by saving him, God was giving him a second chance.

And that's what God does. We too can hide from his purposes for our lives, like Jonah, and he will give us a second chance – but, unlike Jonah, it's best if we listen to him the first time!

(Write on chart.)

1. God called Jonah to a task.
2. Jonah ran off.
3. He ended up seasick, very wet and inside a smelly fish for three days.
4. Jonah agreed to do what God wanted.

Do you really want to go through stages two and three? It could be painful and wasteful. It's better to live in harmony with God's will at all times.

Challenge

How about rereading these first two chapters, then read the last two chapters that will be discussed next week?

Useful resources

http://www.77talksforteens.com/talk53.htm

54
Reading the User's Manual. Part 3

Theme

Reading through the second part of the book of Jonah and considering such topics as God's purposes and his love for the unsaved.

Preparation

OHP/flip chart. Bibles for all.

Discussion

Ask them to list anything they have learned, or key points, from rereading the book of Jonah (if they did actually read it). *(Note them down on chart.)*

Presentation

Jonah's second chance. *(Read Jonah 3:1–2.)*

So God again told Jonah to go and preach to the heathens at Nineveh.

Did he stay or did he go?

He'd learned his lesson and he did what he was told this time.

Jonah's success. *(Read Jonah 3:3–10.)*

Was he the most effective evangelist ever or what?

1. Let's look at the size of the task – it took him three days to travel through the city (and its suburbs) and there were over 120,000 people to be reached. This was no ordinary city – Nineveh was the greatest city of its day.
2. These evil, debauched people actually believed him – even so far as to put on sackcloth and go on a fast – how many of you would have gone that far?
3. The king himself – the most powerful man in the world at that time – turned from his evil ways.

Q: Why did they come through so quickly when it can take us ages just to get one person talking about Jesus?

A: Fear, probably – in verse 4 he predicted that otherwise Nineveh would fall and there must have been sufficient power in his words to drive that point home!

So, Mr Second Chance was given great success. As a man of God, he must have been ecstatically happy at God's great mercy on these people. Let's read on and find out.

Jonah's reaction. *(Read Jonah 4:1–4.)*

Oh dear, what a sour-puss! He was angry at God for being:

- gracious
- compassionate
- slow to anger
- abounding in love
- forgiving.

Had he lost the plot or not? What was the point of three days of evangelising if he didn't want to be successful?

The lesson here is that God can use any of us to achieve his purposes, whatever the state of our heart.

There's the story of a preacher in Wales who was giving a sermon which was an unexpectedly strong one, certainly not one of his usual wishy-washy sermons. He was coming near to the end and suddenly stopped and a strange smile crossed his face. Someone shouted from the congregation, "Look at the preacher, I think he's just gone and converted himself!" God had used him so powerfully that he'd realised through his own preaching that he wasn't right with God!

Discussion

Any testimonies of God working through any members of the group, despite their unwillingness or lack of faith?

Presentation

Q: Jonah's next reaction was curious. Why do you think he wanted to die?

A: Not an easy one. Remember, Jonah was a prophet of Israel, which helps us to understand his reluctance to evangelise the pagans of Nineveh. By seeing how merciful God was to these pagans, Jonah must have thought that God's favour was turning from Israel. This really depressed him.

God then decided that Jonah needed to be shown the error of his ways and we read that next.

Jonah's lesson. *(Read Jonah 4:5–11.)*

What was all that about?

Q: Why do you think that Jonah decided to watch over the city?

A: Because he was still hoping it was going to be destroyed – nice man!

Instead, God was going to teach him a lesson. It was hot, lying there in the sun, so God provided Jonah with a vine to give him shade. But later he sent a worm which destroyed the vine and Jonah was left at the sun's mercy.

And guess what, Jonah got angry again – angry enough to die again!

Was this man ever going to learn?

Q: So what was the purpose of the vine episode?
A: God wanted to show that Jonah was, selfishly, more concerned about the vine – that was given to him as a gift – than he was about the people (and cattle) of Nineveh.

Shame on him! Hopefully he learned from this, though we are not told about his final reaction.

(Read Ezekiel 18:21–23.)

Discussion

What have we learned from the story of Jonah?

1. Never run away from God – but he also gives second chances.
2. God has compassion on everyone, even evil men.
3. We should be willing to spread the gospel to all, even the unlovely.
4. God will use even the unwilling to achieve his purposes.

Useful resources

http://www.77talksforteens.com/talk54.htm

55
SMS Like a Good Idea

Theme

Here we look at the medium, rather than the message, and discover how God took great care in selecting the medium with which to promote his message. We take a look at a modern equivalent, much used by teenagers – SMS, the language of text messaging on mobile phones.

Preparation

Bring along a mobile phone. (Make sure you know its phone number!) Bring some Bibles and an OHP/flip chart.

Presentation

"Je m'appelle . . . . . . Je suis . . . . . ." *(fill in the gaps)*

How many of you understood that? (French for "My name is . . . . . . I am . . . . . .")

If I wanted to tell you my name and occupation, using French ensures that only you French speakers get the facts. English would be far better, wouldn't it?

Now let's travel back 2000 years. Put yourself in God's shoes (sandals?) He had an important message to tell mankind. His Son had come to the world, living among us and teaching us. Then he had died on the cross and returned from the dead to provide a way for us to get right with God.

Q: How could he communicate this vital message not only to those living locally, but to all other people in the world living at that time and in future generations?

A: The written word – manuscripts that can be passed from community to community and read out to large audiences.

But which language?

Hebrew – the religious language in the Holy Land at the time?
Aramaic – the language of the common people at the time?
Latin – the language of the Roman soldiers and officials?
Greek – the language of the eastern Roman empire?

What languages were used in the sign above the cross? Find out in John 19:20.

If God were like us, with our limited vision and understanding, he would have gone the obvious route. Jesus was Jewish, the early disciples were Jewish, the gospel (so they thought at the time) was just for Jews. So . . . let's write it all down in Hebrew or Aramaic.

But . . . the Gospels (the accounts of the life and times of Jesus) were written in Greek.

Why?

Because God saw the wider picture. He knew that all needed to hear the gospel, not just Jews.

So, first, he prepared the scene. Long before, a Greek called Alexander the Great conquered all the known world. Where the Greeks were ruling, most people spoke and understood Greek. After them came the Romans, whose empire spread even further, across Europe to Britain and North Africa. They built roads everywhere and unified their empire in matters of culture, religion and language. So although Latin (the language of Rome) was spoken throughout the empire, Greek was also spoken throughout the Middle East.

So God, through the Romans and Greeks, provided the **way** (the roads) and the **means** (the Greek language) to make sure that any new idea could be spread quickly and efficiently. Even from a little-known and far-flung Roman outpost called Judea in the Middle East, where a man called Paul was preaching about this risen Messiah called Jesus.

God is a God of history – he just doesn't leave us to get on with it! Wasn't he clever? He sets up the scene and allows history to unfold.

Q: If Jesus had instead lived in the twenty-first century, how do you think Christianity would have been spread?
A: Books, TV, e-mail, web, SMS (text messaging).

Let's be more specific. What is the best way, do you think, for a message to be sent to people simultaneously, wherever they are?

Text messaging. Does anyone know who invented it?

It was invented by teenagers in Finland who were too shy to ask each other out on dates face-to-face! Nokia (a Finnish company) noticed this and built it into their mobile phones.

Recently a teenage girl translated Psalm 23 into "text message" language.

(Display on chart) dad@hvn xlnt b ur name

Q: What do you think this (tries to be) the first line of?
A: The Lord's Prayer.

Go to Matthew 6:9–13, a verse at a time. Ask them to pool
their mobile phones (the majority of them will have them) and
to think deeply about each verse and work out the shortest way
to express the verse in SMS. Then they should text it to you
and you write it up on an OHP as soon as you receive one.
Discuss it, then move on to the next verse.

Discussion

Discuss further the ways that information can be sent to as
many people as possible simultaneously. What about those in
poorer countries without access to technology? When Jesus
returns, scripture tells us that we will all know about it at the
same time. Read Matthew 24:30–31 for information.

Challenge

Think about how the medium can affect the message. During
the week see how the various newspapers and radio and TV
coverage report on the same story. Ask yourself why every
story is never told simply, clearly and unemotionally. Why is
there always a slant or "spin"?

Useful resources

http://www.77talksforteens.com/talk55.htm

INKY INDIGO SECTION

Blueprints for Life

56
Why Do the Good Die Young?

Theme

Exploring why God allows some people to die before they have fulfilled their potential.

Preparation

OHP/flip chart. Bibles distributed to all. Pack of cards.

Presentation

Q: What have the following people got in common: Kurt Cobain, Princess Diana, John Lennon, John F. Kennedy and Jesus Christ? *(Add any of your own, if relevant.)*
A: They all died young.

We all know of people who have died young, and it's particularly upsetting when we talk about children or those who had so much to contribute to society.

Christians, too, are not excused and there are plenty of them who have died young – and this is very confusing when you consider that they were all doing God's work. Why did he let them die? Did they do something to anger him? Did they outlive their usefulness?

Q: Cliché time: what is the only thing about life that is 100% certain?
A: That we're all going to die.

And none of us knows when that will be.

Who can play the card game Pontoon?

You turn over cards one after the other, adding up the numbers as you go. The aim is to get the highest total you can, without scoring over 21. If you score too high, then you're **bust**.

(Deal out cards from the pack in the following order – it doesn't matter which suit: 2, 3, 4, 5, 4.)

We have a sum of 18, which is a fair number to stick with – or do we turn over another card? If we turn over a 1, 2 or, especially, a 3, it will be a lot better. If it's any other number, it's bust!

It's like life (if you stretch your mind a little). It approaches a target, but it's basically unpredictable – you never know when you're going to bust.

For non-Christians this is exactly how life is.

(Make a small house out of the cards.)

Piling on the cards until you exceed the target *(destroy the house)* . . . then bust!

For Christians there's a new factor – God. As Christians, it's God who deals the cards.

(Deal out cards from the pack in the following order – it doesn't matter which suit: 2, 3, 4, 5, 4.)

And it is he who decides when to stop, to freeze . . .

(Deal a 7 – of any suit.)

Before it is too late.

To explain, let's read from the Bible.

(Read Isaiah 57:1–2.) "The righteous are taken away to be spared from evil."

(Read Philippians 1:21–24.) ". . . which is better by far."

All we know of is this world, warts and all. It's a fallen world, a flawed world. A world of pain, decay, disappointment, fear, darkness.

Let's look at the world we don't know – heaven.

(Read Revelation 21:1–7.)

Which is better? What is better: 70 or so years here, or an eternity there?

I'm not recommending suicide, as that will not get you to heaven – only God can decide when our number's up.

So when God deals the cards . . .

(Deal out cards from the pack in the following order – it doesn't matter which suit: 2, 3, 4, 5, 4.)

It's he who decides when to stop, because he knows our destination is far better than where we are now.

And perhaps one of the reasons is that he doesn't want this to happen to you.

(Deal a King and hold it up.)

He doesn't want you to be "bust". He wants you with him in paradise. We don't know what this is *(wave card)* – perhaps a falling away from the faith, a major setback, family bereavement . . . but we just have to accept that, for a Christian, when your time's up, your time's up . . . but heaven awaits us.

Can't be bad.

Discussion

There are other considerations (some thorny ones – be prepared):

1. Can you "fall away" from the faith? Once saved always saved?
2. How about those who die without being Christians?
3. How can we best comfort those who mourn?

Useful resources

http://www.77talksforteens.com/talk56.htm

57
Why Do the Downright Rotten (Sometimes) Prosper?

Theme

Again and again we see wicked unbelievers prospering and living to a ripe old age then dying in their sleep. What's the answer? Does God really favour them, or is there more than meets the eye?

Preparation

OHP/flip chart. Bibles distributed to all.

Presentation

Q: What have the following people got in common: Stalin, the Kray brothers, King Herod, Napoleon?
A: They all died at a ripe old age.

The age-old question – why does God allow the wicked to prosper?

For a good old moan read Psalm 73:1–14.

He's right – it's so unfair. Or is it?

Discussion

Are there any drawbacks in living a (non-Christian) life of greed, lust, wickedness, selfishness?

What advantages are there for a Christian life, even if it involves poverty, ill-health, self-sacrifice and danger?

Presentation

So what's the payback? *(Read Psalm 37.)*

Three points:

1. What's better: a comfortable life in this "temporal" world, or an everlasting life in heaven with God?
2. A Christian life frees you from the need to worry about the things the world offers.
3. Remember: you can amass as many riches as you like, but you can't take them with you!

Something else to remember. *(Read Isaiah 57:20–21.)*

Discussion

What should be our response to what we have learned? How can we convince people that they need to change their ways, even if their ways are currently proving so pleasurable for them?

Useful resources

http://www.77talksforteens.com/talk57.htm

58
The True Spirit of Christmas

Theme

A fresh look at Christmas, getting past the smokescreen thrown out by both the secular and the Christian world.

Preparation

OHP/flip chart. Selection of Christmas cards that make no mention of Jesus.

Presentation

This comes from a newspaper dated a few weeks before Christmas 2001:

> "We have great pleasure in inviting you to join us at our sensational new consumer exhibition, Spirit of Christmas, The Ultimate Shopping Experience. Gifts, decorations, food and wine will be offered in a sumptuously decorated Grand Hall at Olympia to create an event with a really unique atmosphere."

The Spirit of Christmas. Let's analyse the word "Christmas" and repeat this phrase.

The spirit of the "remembrance of Jesus Christ".

So when did we get to the point that an occasion for the "remembrance of Christ" becomes an ultimate shopping experience?

Discussion

Note down all the ways that Christmas is celebrated these days, by Christians as well as non-Christians. Mention the fact that, these days, many Christmas cards actually make no mention of the Christmas story. In 2002, one of the major UK card chains admitted that only three out of 960 Christmas cards actually made any mention of the birth of Jesus! *(Show them, if you have any available.)*

Presentation

So let's go back to the beginning. In fact, Christmas goes back further than the birth of Jesus, and the celebration has gone full circle – Christmas has returned to its roots.

And what were these roots?

Well, let's present the ten things you probably didn't know about Christmas. *(Write them on chart.)*

1. It originally had nothing to do with the birth of Jesus.

Q: So when did it start?
A: It was a pagan Roman festival called "Saturnalia", celebrating the birth of the sun god, that fell in December. When Christianity became the state religion, the Christian authorities thought it would be less of a fuss to celebrate the birth of Jesus on a date already used for celebrations – even though they were of a pagan, non-Christian kind. Seemed a good idea at the time.

2. Jesus was probably born in early autumn.

Q: How can we know when he was born?
A: The first clues are that it was unlikely that shepherds would

have had their flocks out in the fields in midwinter, even in Israel. Nor would the Romans have ordered a census in the winter, the most difficult time of the year for travel. There is biblical evidence (see website for details) that Jesus was most likely to have been born in September/October.

3. Jesus was born at least four years "Before Christ".

Q: How can he be born, before he was born?
A: The confusion stems from a monk called Dennis the Short who made mistakes when converting the Roman calendar to a Christian one. His miscalculation wasn't detected until it was too late. A clue was the fact that Herod's census, which was the chief cause of Jesus being born in Bethlehem rather than in his home town of Nazareth, has been confirmed as occurring between 4 and 6 BC.

4. Santa Claus lived in Turkey not Lapland.

Q: How come he lived in Turkey?
A: Well, "Santa Claus" comes from "St Nicholas" – the patron saint of children, as well as merchants and pawnbrokers (or perhaps today's credit card firms!) which seems ironic. St Nick lived in Turkey, so how he ended up in the North Pole is anyone's guess. Mind you, perhaps this is why we eat turkeys at Christmas time!

5. Holly, mistletoe and Christmas trees are not in the Bible.

Q: So where did they come from?
A: Mistletoe has no Christian significance. It's an ancient Druid fertility symbol, and people used to do a lot more than kiss under it. Holly, though connected to Jesus' crown of thorns, has a lot more to do with the god Saturn and the old pagan holly king. Evergreen trees were a potent symbol of life in the dark winter days. Decorating them was a way

268 77 TALKS FOR BORED-AGAIN TEENAGERS

of making offerings to the tree's spirit, which you will find nowhere in the Bible, except as a pagan practice that cursed you with death and other judgements.

6. Jesus was not born in a stable.

Q: So where was he born?

A: The inn mentioned in the Bible was not a hotel as we know it. It was an open hall, probably with a table around which the guests reclined to eat and drink, then lay there around the table to sleep. It was very public, very busy and probably very noisy, somewhat like a bus terminal. The stable, on the other hand, was most likely a cave, not a barn or shed. Therefore, it would have been warm and dry, and, most importantly, private.

7. The wise men gave no gifts to the baby Jesus.

Q: So what did they give?

A: They gave gifts – gold, frankincense and myrrh – but not to the baby Jesus, rather to the infant Jesus, who may have been two years old at the time. Nativity scenes tend to oversimplify the events, but a careful reading tells us that the wise men visited Jesus as a "child" in a "house".

8. And there weren't three wise men, anyway.

Q: Then who gave the gifts?

A: Another example of traditions obscuring the truth. Three gifts are mentioned, but nowhere does it say that there were only **three** of these wise men!

9. Boxing Day has no religious meaning.

Q: So where did it come from?

A: St Stephen's Day (26 December) was the traditional

occasion when the charity boxes in churches were opened and the money distributed to the poor of the parish. In Victorian times the custom was enlarged to allow servants a day's holiday to visit their families, as cooks, maids, butlers, grooms, etc. would have had to work on Christmas Day to ensure that the gentry had a splendid time.

10. No one in the Bible actually ate Christmas pudding.

Q: How can you say that?

A: The formula wasn't around in those days. Traditionally the stirring of the pud takes place at the beginning of Advent on "stir-up Sunday". Each family member would give the pudding mixture a stir while making a secret wish. Stirring should be done in an east to west direction to commemorate the visit of the Wise Men. This of course is totally biblical . . . not!

Discussion

We know three things about Christmas.

- It has pagan roots.
- Most Christmas traditions are at worst pagan, and at best are biblical corruptions.
- Commercialism has obscured the true message of Christmas.

So should we celebrate it? If so, how best can we celebrate it so that it has a clear Christian message and meaning?

(If there is time you may want to read the Christmas story, just to close: Luke 1:5–80; Matthew 1:18–25; Luke 2:1–38; Matthew 2.)

Useful resources

http://www.77talksforteens.com/talk58.htm

59
It's All in the Name

Theme

A look at names in the Bible and what we can learn from them.

Preparation

OHP/flip chart. If possible get a list of first names of the attendees and use a names dictionary to note down the meaning of these names. Bibles for all. Paper and pens.

Presentation

(Read out the list of name meanings and get the audience to guess who is referred to, with a short discussion as to whether that person's character fits with the description.)

So what's in a name? Does it have any use other than being a way of telling us apart?

Well, in the Bible, we find there's a lot we can learn from people's names.

Q: Let's first look at the third Jewish Patriarch – who was?
A: Jacob.
Q: Which means?
A: An interesting one as there are two possible answers. One meaning referred to the manner of his birth and the other referred to his character. Depending on your source, Jacob could either mean **heel-grabber** *(read Genesis 25:24–26)* or **deceiver** *(read Genesis 27:34–36). (Write on chart.)*

Jacob cheated Esau out of his inheritance as the first-born. But Jacob was still the chosen one of God and even had a wrestling match with him! Jacob survived the bout with the Almighty resulting in, for him, a new name. *(Read Genesis 32:24–28.)*

His name was now **Israel**, which means "He struggles with God". *(Write on chart.)*

In the book of Ruth, we find that Naomi (whose names meant "my pleasant one") changed her name to **Marah** ("Bitter") after her troubles.

Now, did you know that God himself has a name? Moses asked him his name in Exodus 3:13–14. *(Read it.)*

This is a simplified version of his real name that could never be spoken out loud or, according to legend, the world will come to an end!

But his name, in its simplified form, indicates in some way the awesomeness and majesty of God – "I am who I am" – it sort of implies, "Hey, I know who I am, who are you to ask?!" *(Write on chart.)*

Then there's the name that is so major that it was used to create the universe and provides the seal of approval for our prayers.

Q: And what name is this?
A: Jesus.

Right . . . and wrong.

This is correct inasmuch as Jesus is the name that we use for the Son of God, the person who died on the cross for our sins.

But Jesus **wasn't** his name. It is by knowing his real name that we can get a real understanding of his mission on earth.

Let's start at the beginning . . .

"The Virgin Mary was pregnant" . . . **wrong!**

There was no one in those days called "Mary". "Mary" is an English name, but we're talking about Jews living in Israel.

Her name was **Miriam** . . . not Mary. That was her **Hebrew** name. And her name meant "God's gift". *(Write on chart.)*

"And Miriam gave birth to Jesus" . . . **wrong!**

His name wasn't Jesus, it was **Yeshua**. That was the name he was known by. That was his **Hebrew** name – Jesus is just the English translation of his Hebrew name. *(Write on chart.)*

"So what?" you may say. "He knows who we're talking about when we talk about Jesus, so why confuse us with this **Yeshua** business?"

There's a good reason for this, because everyone who knew him as **Yeshua**, also knew what the word meant.

Q: So what does **Yeshua** mean?
A: Salvation. *(Write on chart.)*

(Read Matthew 1:21.)

Let's face it, this doesn't **really** mean anything to us.

Yet, if, instead of the name of **Jesus**, we use the name **Yeshua**, or, even better, the word **salvation**, which is the meaning of the word Yeshua . . . then . . .

(Read Matthew 1:21 – substituting "salvation" for the word "Jesus".)

Do you get my point? We now see what's meant here.

But God gave him this name Yeshua for another reason. The name itself was to be a witness to the Jewish people of his day, who understood the Old Testament.

Because every time the word "salvation" appeared in the Old Testament – which is in quite a few places – the word used would be **Yeshua** – Jesus.

They couldn't avoid the word Jesus – it's all over the Old Testament!

(Read Psalm 9:14, Genesis 49:18, Psalm 91:14–16, Isaiah 12:2–3, Isaiah 62:11, etc. In each of these, substitute the word Jesus every time you see "salvation".)

So we can learn much from names in the Bible.

Discussion

Give out pens and paper and get them to rename other members of the group according to their qualities. See if you get agreement in the group. Perhaps look at people's nicknames and analyse how they got them.

Useful resources

http://www.77talksforteens.com/talk59.htm

60
The Three Rubber Bands

Theme

A look at the three things that try to pull us back to our old ways – the world, the flesh and the devil.

Preparation

OHP/flip chart. Three long pieces of string (about three metres long each), two chairs, five labels. Questionnaires, pens, ballot box.

Presentation

Does anyone here like burgers? Fries? Milk shakes?

If you ask the big companies about the nutritional value of their meals, they'll say they're good for you. There's protein in the burgers, and vitamins in the salad and the milk shakes. What they don't say is that there's so much fat in them that people in the USA are suing the companies, saying it's their fault that a whole generation of kids are obese.

Moral: Not everything that **seems** to be good for you, **is** good for you.

When you become a Christian, you have to start thinking about such things. It's not easy being a Christian and there's plenty out there that's going to try and return you to your old ways.

We need three volunteers.

*(Attach a piece of string to each volunteer and get them to stand in a line, about a metre apart from each other. Attach the other end of each piece of string to a chair about three metres away on their left. Put a label on this chair "**Old ways**". Place another chair to the right of the volunteers and label it "**New creation – 2 Corinthians 5:17**".)*

Let's pretend these strings are pieces of elastic. They exist to pull us, the new creation, back into our old ways. We can see **three things** which can pull us back. Let's look at them now:

The world. *(Put "the world" label on first volunteer.)* So how does the world pull us back? Let's see what the Bible says. *(Read John 15:19.)*

So we don't belong to the world any more – but the world wants us back. So it entices us with distractions and amusements.

(Give out pens and "the world" questionnaires, which should look like the one below.)

Music	☐
Film	☐
TV	☐
Books/magazines	☐
Politics	☐

I'd like you to be honest and think about each of these in turn. Have any of these ever dragged you back a little in your Christian life? Think how they may have exposed you to trivial content, sexual or violent images, the occult, horror, blasphemy, or bad behaviour. If that's the case, just tick the box – it's anonymous.

(Collect the slips in the ballot box and look at them: if more than half the people have ticked any particular box, ask "the world" volunteer to step one pace closer to the "old ways" chair.)

So the influence of "the world" has proved attractive to some of us.

The flesh. *(Put "the flesh" label on second volunteer.)*

The flesh? Strange word – conjures up images of a butcher's shop or a strip show. Matthew 26:41 tells us, "the spirit is willing but the **flesh is weak**." (RSV)

Q: So it's a part of us that we find hard to control – any suggestions here? A further clue is in Romans 7:5. "While we were living in the flesh, our sinful passions, aroused by the law, were at work in our members to bear fruit for death." (RSV)

A: Answers should include variations on the seven deadly sins – pride, envy, greed, lust, anger, gluttony, sloth (laziness).

So how do we rate with "the flesh"?

(Give out "the flesh" questionnaires, which should look like "the world" but use the categories of pride, envy, greed, lust, anger, gluttony, laziness.)

Now again I want you to be honest and tick the box of any of these seven deadly sins of the flesh that have dragged you back a little (or a lot) in your Christian life. If you have had difficulties in any of these areas, tick the box – it's anonymous.

(Collect the slips as before and count results. If more than half the people have ticked any particular box, ask "the flesh" volunteer to step one pace closer to the "old ways" chair.)

So the weaknesses of "the flesh" have proved a problem to some of us.

The devil. *(Put "the devil" label on third volunteer.)*

The devil – a real person, a very real influence. There's no time to give you the full rundown on this particular person, except to admit that he can be a real pain in the backside and, like an attack of the measles, can be dangerous if ignored.

Before Jesus came along in your life, this was the one you followed, whether you liked it or not, whether you knew it or not!

(Read 1 Peter 5:8.) "The devil prowls around like a roaring lion, seeking some one to devour." (RSV)

So he's constantly prowling around, looking for weaknesses. He particularly hates Christians because he knows he has lost them and is, at the end of the day, through the authority of Jesus, powerless against them.

But he can still cause damage. One way is through temptation. He could whisper things to you like, "Call yourself a Christian? I saw you staring at those legs!" or "Go on, take it, they're insured!"

No Christian is spared from this, but it may be well to memorise the following verse, from 1 Corinthians 10:13:

"No temptation has seized you except what is common to man. And God is faithful; he will not let you be tempted beyond what you can bear. But when you are tempted, he will also provide a way out so that you can stand up under it."

Hold on to that promise. It works!

(Give out paper.)

Now again I want you to be honest and just write one word in answer to this question: "Have I ever been tempted in any way since I've become a Christian?" Use one of the following words: never, sometimes, quite often, a lot.

(Put slips into ballot box and then collect them and according to the type of answers, make the "devil" volunteer step some paces closer to the chair marked with "old ways".)

So, if we're honest, we've all been tempted by the devil.

Discussion

See how far our volunteers have been pulled back to the "old ways". How can we fight against it? Look for answers like self-control, self-censorship, self-discipline, Bible reading, prayer, fellowship.

Useful resources

http://www.77talksforteens.com/talk60.htm

61
Intercessor Extraordinaire

Theme

A look at the life and times of Rees Howells.

Preparation

Four extracts on separate sheets of paper for people to read out.

Presentation

There's praying . . . and there's **praying**.

There's the . . . *(close eyes and put hands together)* . . . "Please God, look after my mum and dad and brother and my cat Mitzi and give me a good day and keep that bully away from me . . ." – type prayer.

Contrast that with the following example.

This was prayer for a man called Rees Howells. He was a Christian, born in a poor Welsh mining village at the end of the nineteenth century. He was a man so soaked in prayer and intercession that he was even able to influence world events.

This is his story and there's a lot we can learn from the life of a Christian who really took prayer **seriously**. Let's find out more by reading key moments in his life.

(Distribute following four conversations to four volunteers.)

He was already a Christian when he first started getting serious with God after coming back from a meeting.

Conversation 1

"I was in a train going to a Christian meeting when a voice spoke to me 'When you return, you will be a new man.' 'But I am a new man!' 'No, you are a child.' On the first morning of the Convention the preacher spoke on Ephesians 2:1–6. 'You hath he quickened . . . and hath raised us up . . . and made us sit together in heavenly places in Christ Jesus.' He then asked the question, 'Have you been quickened by Christ? Have you been raised up to sit with Him in heavenly places?' In my heart I answered, 'Yes, I know I have been quickened, but I have not been raised up with Christ to that place of power'. The moment I said that, I saw the Glorified Christ, and the same voice I had heard in the train said to me, 'Would you like to sit there with Him? There is a place for you'. I saw myself raised up with Him. I knew now what it meant to be 'glorified'. All that night I was in the presence of God and my glorified Saviour. There is nothing in nature refined enough to describe it."

Discussion

Just because such experiences are rare these days, do we doubt them? Why do we think such experiences are rare? Has anyone here heard of similar experiences?

Conversation 2

"God made it very plain that He would never share my life. I saw the honour He gave me in offering to indwell me, but there were many things very dear to me, and I know He wouldn't keep one of them. The change He would make was very clear. It meant every bit of my fallen nature was to go to the cross, and he would bring in His own life and His own nature. It was unconditional surrender. From the meeting I went out into a field where I cried my heart out because I had lived in my body for twenty-six years, and could I easily give it up? I intended to do it, but oh, the cost! I wept for days. I lost seven pounds in weight, just because I saw what He was offering me. But I had to give up everything – my love for money, personal ambition, love of food."

Discussion

Would we be willing to give up everything we hold dear if God told us it was necessary for a closer walk with him?

Presentation

Rees Howells was called to a life of intense intercession, often praying through the night on a single topic. God challenged him with tramps, drunkards and unlovely people. He had to pray them all into the kingdom, often at great cost to himself and to his reputation. In one instance he had to pray for a woman without ever meeting her. God told him to pray for her for months, with the promise that, if he did, she would become a Christian by Christmas. He did and on Christmas day she gave her life to God.

Conversation 3

"I spoke at a meeting and was asked to define what I do. I explained that I wasn't what they call a prayer warrior, who would pray for something but would not necessarily expect the answer to come through themselves. It is different for us intercessors. We are responsible to see the prayer through and would never be free until it is. We would go through every length for the prayer to be answered through ourselves.

But once a position of intercession has been gained, tested and proved, the intercessor can claim all the blessings."

Rees Howells would often do a full day's work in the mines, then be on his knees for three hours every evening.

Discussion

Is it easier or harder for a Christian to have such a calling these days?

Presentation

He was soon given an international ministry. He prayed for poor widows in India and missions in Africa, where he also worked for a while as a missionary, before founding a Bible college in Wales, which was responsible for sending thousands of missionaries out into the world. It came into its own, though, during the Second World War. Here is his account of the Battle of Britain in 1940.

Conversation 4

"The situation was grim. The Nazis' air force was far greater than ours in numbers. We could hear the planes over the college as we prayed and interceded for our brave pilots. I trusted God for our protection during those times and not a bomb touched us, although all around us they fell. The situation in the country because of air raids may become very serious. We have never walked this way before. The peace that our Saviour gives us is not an artificial one, it is so deep that the devil can't disturb it. On September 8th as I led the mid-day service we could hear Nazi planes overhead, yet I knew they would not touch us. We sang songs of victory. There was no need to pray any more for protection, the Holy Ghost came down on us in that meeting and told us of His victory! We prayed hard for London, which was being heavily bombed and, at all times, I knew we had the victory."

Presentation

After the war Winston Churchill spoke of that battle, "I asked the Air Marshal what reserves we had of planes and he said 'None'. Yet five minutes afterwards suddenly it seemed that the German planes just gave up. No more attacks. Then ten minutes later the action ended. There seemed no earthly reason for this. They just went home at the moment when victory was in their grasp." The Air Chief Marshal also spoke, "Even during the battle one realised from day to day how much external support was coming in. At the end of the battle one had the sort of feeling that there had been some special divine intervention to alter some sequence of events which otherwise would have occurred."

Such is the power of prayer.

Discussion

Do we believe that prayer can influence world events? If so, why don't we pray more? Perhaps the group can set up a prayer group to pray for the world and the country.

Useful resources

http://www.77talksforteens.com/talk61.htm
The conversations in this talk are taken from *Rees Howells, Intercessor* by Norman Grubb (Lutterworth Press).

62
Sanctity of Life:
When Death Beckons

Theme

A look at the value of life from the perspective of someone near death. Euthanasia is looked at from a Christian perspective.

Preparation

OHP/flip chart.

Presentation

A lady is dying from motor neurone disease, an incurable illness which has wasted her muscles. She is confined to a wheelchair, scarcely able to speak and fed through a tube; the prospect that lies before her is progressive suffocation as her breathing and swallowing muscles fail. Yet her mind remains clear. She wishes to die before her illness becomes intolerable, with her family around her, at home, in a manner and at a time of her own choosing. If she could move just one arm, she could commit suicide. But she cannot move; everything now has to be done for her. That means she cannot carry out her desire to die unless someone helps her.

Discussion

Should her husband be allowed to help her to commit suicide? (One minute discussion.)

Presentation

She went to the High Court for permission to get help from her husband to help her to die. The High Court refused.

No doubt if she was able to commit suicide, the law would have let her (through the 1961 Suicide Act), but if her husband or anyone else helps her, then it is murder and he would be prosecuted.

The issue here is **euthanasia** – also called "assisted suicide". *(Write on chart.)*

How should we feel as Christians?

- On the one hand, she was in pain and had no hope: surely to help her end it all would be an act of love.
- On the other hand, murder is murder whatever the circumstances.

If she had lived in The Netherlands or the US state of Oregon there would have been no problems, as euthanasia is legal there.

Q: What does euthanasia mean?
A: A "good" death.

What's a good death? What's a bad death? What's death?

A big subject.

Job, the man who was so afflicted in the Old Testament, talked to God about human beings.

"Man's days are determined; you have decreed the number of his months and have set limits he cannot exceed." *(Job 14:5)*

And that's basically all there is to say on the subject for a Christian, it's here in black and white. God's in charge. He and only he decides when we die, whatever the circumstances.

Even if Job, in his desperation cried out, "Why did I not perish at birth, and die as I came from the womb?" *(Job 3:11)*

There are so many issues to euthanasia. To care for a dying relative or friend must be heart-wrenching, but the fact remains that there is a better life to come after death for a Christian, and our duty to that loved one should be to communicate that fact to them.

The other important fact is to remember again what Job said: God decides. Just because it **seems** that someone's life is near its end doesn't mean that God is of the same opinion. He has full control of our lives. He is a God of healing and, if he so plans, can heal anyone in any situation.

"There is no God besides me. I put to death and I bring to life." *(Deuteronomy 32:39)*

Prayer

Father, help us to be people of your word, proclaiming your truths to a world that denies them. Help us to be bold in this difficult area, coping with any situation that we may be exposed to. Help us to be loving and not judgemental, loving the sick, not just in our actions and attitude, but in our desire to help them receive your gift of eternal life that you give freely to all who ask.

Useful resources

http://www.77talksforteens.com/talk62.htm

63
Holy Communion, Batman!

Theme

Understanding Holy Communion through a dramatic reconstruction of its origins in the Last Supper.

Preparation

Photocopies of the script, for different people to read. You can even have a meal first, and read the drama after the meal, for extra authenticity. It would be good to use authentic Jewish matzah (unleavened) bread and some red wine (or blackcurrant juice).

Presentation

It's called a lot of different things: Holy Communion, The Eucharist, Mass, the Lord's Supper.

You've all seen it, some of you have taken part in it. But what is it?

Christianity is a **historical** faith: everything it teaches goes back to a single event in history. The same with Holy Communion. So let's set the scene.

It's the night before Jesus' crucifixion. He is enjoying a Jewish Passover meal with his disciples, his Last Supper. After this meal he is to go to the Garden of Gethsemane, where he will be betrayed, brought to trial and crucified. We are going to re-enact what probably happened towards the end of that meal, piecing together what is written in the Bible with what actually happens in a Jewish Passover service.

(Read Matthew 26:17–30.)

We start. We read from 1 Corinthians, Chapter 11:23–26.

BIBLE READER: For I received from the Lord the teaching that I
                 passed on to you: that the Lord Jesus, on the
                 night he was betrayed, took a piece of bread . . .
NARRATOR: The meal is over. Jesus reaches out and takes a
                 piece of unleavened bread that had been
                 wrapped in a linen cloth. This piece, called the
                 afikoman, was broken off from a larger piece of
                 bread earlier in the service, as part of the ritual.
                 It was wrapped and hidden, waiting for its
                 recovery after the meal. The time had now
                 come.
BIBLE READER: . . . he gave thanks to God . . .
JESUS: Blessed are you, O Lord our God, ruler of the
                 universe, who brings forth bread from the
                 earth.
BIBLE READER: . . . he broke the bread . . .
JESUS: This is my body, which is broken for you.
PETER: What do you mean? How can this bread be . . .
                 your body?
JESUS: *(holding bread)* See this bread. It has no leaven,
                 no yeast. Have you thought of the significance?
JOHN: Yes, of course, master. Our forefathers had to
                 leave Egypt in a hurry, there was no time for
                 the bread to rise.
JESUS: True. But what have I taught you about yeast?
MATTHEW: Beware of the yeast of the Pharisees, the
                 Sadducees and of Herod!
JESUS: Well remembered, Matthew. One day you'll
                 have to write these things down!
PETER: You were talking of their hearts, weren't you,
                 their wickedness?
JESUS: Wickedness, hypocrisy, malice, all of these

things. This is why, when you think of me, you think of this bread without yeast, without malice, without wickedness . . . without sin.

JOHN: Yes, Master, this bread will remind us of you. But you're not going anywhere . . . are you . . . ?
(pause)
(Jesus breaks the bread and distributes it to the others. All eat.)

NARRATOR: During the Passover meal there are four cups of wine drunk. Each has a different meaning. The first two, the cups of blessing and judgement, have already been drunk before the meal. Jesus now lifts the third cup, the cup of redemption.

BIBLE READER: In the same way, after the supper he took the cup . . .

JESUS: Blessed are you, O Lord our God, ruler of the universe, who creates the fruit of the vine.

BIBLE READER: . . . then he said . . .

JESUS: This cup is God's new covenant, sealed with my blood.

PETER: New covenant? Your blood? Master, what's this all about?

JOHN: Quiet, Peter, I'm sure if we weren't so thick we would have figured it out!

JESUS: John, you show great modesty, that's a real "Revelation". But these are new concepts for you all. Just understand that I am starting something new here tonight, for you and for the world. Tomorrow I go to be sacrificed, my blood to be shed.

PETER: Surely not, Master. I will not allow this!

JESUS: Peter! We've talked before about this. You must think before you speak! My mission is for all mankind. Are you to be a hindrance?

PETER: I'm sorry, Master.

JESUS: Whenever you drink this "cup of redemption",

do so in memory of me. Up to now you have
taken this cup to remind you of God's
redemption of your forefathers at that first
Passover under Moses. But from now on, this
cup will remind you of my blood to be shed.
(All drink from their cup.)

NARRATOR: And so was instituted Holy Communion.
Passover was a festival of remembrance, a time
to remember the physical salvation of the Jews
at the time of the Exodus. Jesus used this very
festival to create a new act of remembrance, the
taking of bread and wine by Christians ever
since, to remember our spiritual salvation
through the broken body and the shed blood of
Jesus Christ.

Discussion

Discuss the practices of the group. Are they all Christians and
do they all take Holy Communion? If not, why not? If so, why?
Do they still have questions or objections? It may be worth
reading 1 Corinthians 11:17–33, regarding conduct when
partaking of Holy Communion.

Useful resources

http://www.77talksforteens.com/talk63.htm

64
And You Thought You Were Bad!

Theme

An overview of some of the major characters in the Bible, showing them to be flesh and blood and just as flawed as we are.

Preparation

OHP/flip chart.

Presentation

(Write the following on chart.)

J. R. Ewing, Homer Simpson, Darth Vader, Hannibal Lecter, Norman Bates, Goldfinger.

Q: What do this sorry lot have in common?
A: Deeply flawed individuals (or words to that effect).

Contrast them with this list:

(Write the following on chart.)

Adam, Noah, Abraham, Jacob, Moses, David, Paul, Peter.

What a contrast! . . . **wrong**!

(Write the following words next to each name. See if they can find the Bible verses that prove each point. Answers are given in brackets.)

- Adam – failure *(Genesis 3:17–19)*
- Noah – drunk *(Genesis 9:21)*
- Abraham – coward *(Genesis 20:11)*
- Jacob – cheat *(Genesis 27:19)*
- Moses – murderer *(Exodus 2:12)*
- David – adulterer *(2 Samuel 11:4)*
- Peter – liar *(Matthew 26:70)*
- John and James the disciples – big-heads *(Matthew 20:22)*

But there is a difference between our second list and the first. At least the Bible characters had **some** redeeming qualities – otherwise how could God have used them at all?

(Ask them to come up with positive qualities and write them next to each name – they may need some help.)

- Adam – obedient (eventually)
- Noah – righteous, patient, godly
- Abraham – faithful, leader, father
- Jacob – remorseful, resourceful
- Moses – leader, deliverer, law-giver, sacrificial
- David – brave, deliverer, poet, faithful
- Peter – loyal (eventually), leader
- John the apostle – friend, loyal

So, the Bible is the story of flawed human beings.

It is also the story of how God still used them, despite their flaws! *(Read 2 Corinthians 4:7–10.)*

God doesn't want us to be perfect, just **available**.

Tell him you're available and see what he will do with your life.

Useful resources

http://www.77talksforteens.com/talk64.htm

65
Spread it about

Theme

Illustrating the importance of evangelism.

Preparation

OHP/flip chart. Some tracts to give out.

Presentation

There's an urban legend going around.

> "There's a group of people dotted around the world who have been visited by an extra-terrestrial and have been shown awesome secrets and promised an exciting future. They have also been told to tell others about their good fortune. But most don't do it and live their lives guarding this knowledge but, by doing so, condemn others to live without purpose."

I lied – this is not an urban legend but rather Christian reality.

We have this awesome secret – it is the gospel of Jesus Christ!

The **reality** is this: if every Christian were effective in communicating the Gospel message to just **one person** every year, the number of Christians in the world would **double** every year!

Yet every year the actual growth is around 2–3%, and even less in the Western world.

What this means is: an average church (of around 100 people) would expect just two or three new converts every year. Pretty pathetic really.

So how important is it for us to communicate the gospel?

I'll just give two reasons: *(Write on chart.)*

1. Because Jesus told us to. *(Read Matthew 28:19.)*
2. Otherwise you could be condemning your non-Christian loved ones to this. *(Read 2 Thessalonians 1:8–10.)*

So think about it!

So where do we start?

(Read 1 Peter 3:15–16. Read it slowly and together.)

Always be prepared . . .

Discussion

*   When is a good time, when is a bad time . . . to give an answer to everyone who asks you?
*   Would you be willing to share your faith with everyone who asks you, enemies and strangers as well as friends and family . . . to give the reason for the hope that you have?
*   Do we have enough experience and the knowledge to share the gospel?

A good point.

How did we become Christians?

- A gradual experience through having a Christian upbringing? *(Ask for a show of hands.)*

Q: Do you consider that you have enough Christian knowledge to talk of your faith through what you learned at Sunday School or what you've been taught at school?

- A definite single conversion experience? *(Ask for a show of hands.)*

Q: You were sufficiently convinced by the witness of someone else to become a Christian. Could you not do the same for another?

Presentation

What about the experience of the secret ingredient . . . the Holy Spirit?

(Read 1 Corinthians 2:4–5.)

Prayer

Heavenly Father, may we be ready at all times to tell others of the hope we have as Christians. Send us your Holy Spirit to give us both the opportunity to share our faith and the words by which to do so. Amen.

Challenge

Give out relevant tracts. Challenge God to give you an opportunity for witness over the next week. Make sure that you are equipped to do so and, if relevant to you, familiarise yourself with the tract. Be prepared to share your experiences next week.

Useful resources

http://www.77talksforteens.com/talk65.htm

66
That Amazing Grace!

Theme

Using the words of the famous song, we look at the subject of God's undeserved grace.

Preparation

OHP/flip chart. Recording of "Amazing grace" and musical equipment and (preferably) a guitar and guitarist with the music. Distribute lyrics.

Presentation

(Play song.)

This song is probably the most famous and most recorded Christian hymn of all time – it has been covered by all types of music groups, from Scottish bagpipe ensembles to native American flutes. It's been used on TV adverts and even accompanied floor exercises in the 1996 Olympic Games!

It was written in the eighteenth century by John Newton, a colourful character who had been an English slave in Africa before becoming a slave trader himself. A right scoundrel! Someone who, when he became a Christian, was making a life-change more drastic than most!

(Play and sing first verse together. Display lyrics.)

Amazing grace! How sweet the sound
That saved a wretch like me!

I once was lost, but now am found;
Was blind, but now I see.

The first thing we should ask is – what is **grace**?

There are eleven possible meanings – so, the first question is, which one is so amazing that a hymn can be written about it?

Which meaning of "grace" are we talking about? Hands up please:

- Effortless beauty or charm.
- A characteristic or quality pleasing for its charm or refinement.
- A sense of fitness.
- A generous or helpful person.
- A temporary immunity or reprieve.
- A Greek goddess.
- A girl's name.
- A short prayer of blessing before or after a meal.
- A sixteenth-century English musical term.
- A title for a duke or archbishop.
- A sense of divine favour.

Our amazing grace = a sense of divine favour – something God gives us when we become a Christian *(write on chart)*.

John Newton called it **amazing** grace because God was even willing to save "such a wretch as he", to find such a "lost soul" and to give him "spiritual sight".

The fact is that, without grace from God – we are lost!

(Read Romans 6:23, Ephesians, 2:4–5.)

On the basis of our sins we are dead, but because of God's grace – a free gift – we have eternal life.

Grace is what keeps the whole thing going, like a continuous flow of oil keeping the cogs and gears of our salvation operational.

There is no obligation for God to be like this – we certainly do not deserve it. God does it because he loves us.

But there are other aspects of God's grace.

(Play and sing second verse together.)

'Twas grace that taught my heart to fear,
And grace my fears relieved;
How precious did that grace appear
The hour I first believed.

Discussion

What does this verse tell us about grace? What is the difference between grace and the actions of the Holy Spirit? *(Write key conclusions on chart.)*

Presentation

(Play and sing third verse together.)

Through many dangers, toils and snares,
I have already come;
'Tis grace hath brought me safe thus far,
And grace will lead me home.

Discussion

What does this verse tell us about grace? Is grace operational
before we become a Christian? *(Write key conclusions on
chart.)*

Presentation

(Play and sing fourth verse together.)

The Lord has promised good to me,
His Word my hope secures;
He will my Shield and Portion be,
As long as life endures.

Discussion

What does this verse tell us about grace? Do we continue in
grace after we become a Christian? *(Write key conclusions on
chart.)*

Presentation

(Play and sing remaining verses together.)

Yea, when this flesh and heart shall fail,
And mortal life shall cease,
I shall possess, within the veil,
A life of joy and peace.

The Earth shall soon dissolve like snow,
The sun forbear to shine;
But God, Who called me here below,
Shall be forever mine.

When we've been there ten thousand years,
Bright shining as the sun,
We've no less days to sing God's praise
Than when we'd first begun.

A glorious future for us as Christians, and all because of grace
– a free gift from God to us.

Useful resources

http://www.77talksforteens.com/talk66.htm

PARMA VIOLET SECTION

Solid Food

67
A Day in the Life of Jesus: a Leper Healed

Theme

An examination of Luke 5:12–16.

Preparation

Bibles for all, OHP/flip chart.

Presentation

Q: These days, who do we treat like "lepers"?
A: HIV/AIDs sufferers, facial deformed, mentally handicapped.

Key factors are:

- We find it hard to look at people who are physically different.
- We are worried about catching a disease.

At the time of Jesus, leprosy had both of these factors. It was the worst thing that could happen to you.

According to the holy writings you were made "unclean" by touching an "unclean" animal like a pig or a dead body, human or otherwise. The only other way to become "unclean" was by touching a leper.

(Write following on chart.)

- If you touch a leper you become "unclean".
- If you touch a leper, there's a good chance of becoming one too.
- Lepers are as they are supposedly because of some terrible sin they have committed.

Being a leper used to be bad news. Talking to one was bad, in fact you were meant to stay at least six feet away and certainly not downwind! Touching one was considered sheer madness.

(Read Luke 5:12–16.)

A man came along who was covered with leprosy.

Jesus talked to him, touched him . . . and healed him!

Q: What did the leper have to show in order to be healed?
A: Faith.

Note that the leper first had to have faith before Jesus could perform his miracle. The leper had to believe that Jesus could do it, before he actually did it.

Now leprosy was a strange disease. Since the time of Moses, no Jew had **ever** been cured of leprosy. There was no cure known by doctors or religious leaders. In fact, according to their holy writings, only **one** person could ever heal a leper – the Messiah who was to come, the anointed one, the Christ.

Jesus did something very special here. He was throwing down the gauntlet to the religious authorities. He was saying this:

"Hey, you don't want to believe in me, but you're going to have to now. I've just done something that no mere man could ever do. I've performed a miracle that you say only the Messiah could do. So what does that make me?"

Yet although there was no known cure, the Book of Leviticus (Leviticus 13–14) gave lots of details of what to do **if** a leper was healed. It was as if Moses (who wrote this book) knew that one day, in the future, one would come who would be able to cure this disease.

This is what Leviticus tells us. If someone claimed to be healed of leprosy he had to go to the priests and: *(write following on chart)*

- Offer a sacrifice of two birds.
- Start a seven-day investigation to answer three questions:
  1. Was the person really a leper?
  2. Was he actually cured of leprosy?
  3. How did he get cured?
- Offer a whole series of sacrifices on the eighth day.

The only possible conclusion they could make in this case was that Jesus **had** to be the Messiah.

So Jesus told the ex-leper to go off to the religious authorities for this eight-day examination and purification.

Because the whole episode would be "a testimony to them".

Q: If you were one of these religious leaders and someone came along claiming to be the very person that your religion has been longing for for over 1000 years what would you do?

A: Take notice and have him followed.

And this is why we read that crowds of people now came to seek Jesus out, to listen to him and to be healed by him. You can imagine that a lot of these would be spies sent by the religious authorities to check him out.

Discussion

If Jesus came today and performed a miracle that modern science proclaimed impossible, how would our leaders cope with this? Would they accept Jesus' claims about himself or would they try and discredit him? Jesus threatened the "status quo" of his day. Have things really changed?

Prayer

Thank you, Lord, for showing us illustrations in your word that illuminate different aspects of Jesus' character and mission. We thank you for the compassion that he showed this leper in healing him and, by doing so, helped many others towards an understanding of who exactly he was, the promised Christ, the saviour of the world.

Useful resources

http://www.77talksforteens.com/talk67.htm

68
A Day in the Life of Jesus: Healing the Paralytic

Theme

An examination of Luke 5:17–26.

Preparation

Bibles for all, OHP/flip chart.

Presentation

In the last session we saw Jesus defying every convention in the book by speaking to, touching and healing a leper. By doing so he was signaling his credentials to the religious authorities of the day – only the Messiah could do what he'd just did! The result of this was that the religious authorities would now send spies to this new teacher to check him out.

(Read Luke 5:17.)

There's a particular TV programme that appears now and again. It's called "An audience with . . ." and has featured such luminaries as Kylie Minogue, Jackie Mason and Rod Stewart. The idea is that the "celebrity" does their thing on stage to an audience of their peers, the great and the good of the entertainment industry, who are there to pay homage and be entertained. Everyone has a good time and there's plenty of back slapping.

It was not so for Jesus. Here were gathered teachers, preachers, priests and scribes from all over the land. They were there, **not** to pay homage, but to watch and take notes.

(Read Luke 5:18–19.)

Picture the scene. Jesus was in a house "chilling out".
Meanwhile a paralysed man was lying on a mat carried by his friends. They approached the house and realised that, due to the large crowd, there was no way into the house – all entrances were blocked. No room to get in!

Some would have given up. Not this lot. They climbed on the roof of the house, removed a few tiles and lowered their friend down.

Q: What qualities were these men showing by their actions?
A: Persistence, faith, friendship, desperation.

(Read Luke 5:20.)

In this one utterance Jesus was saying different things to different people.

• To the paralytic and his friends, he commended their faith – they took so much trouble getting there, they must have **really** believed that Jesus was going to heal.
• To the paralytic he didn't heal him at that instant – he forgave his sins!
• To the religious observers (spies) among the assembled crowd, he was making a **major statement**!

To understand the last two points better read Psalm 103:1–3.

Q: According to the psalm (and in many other places in the Old Testament), who is the only one who can forgive sins?

A: God.
Q: But who was forgiving sins in the Luke passage?
A: Jesus.
Q: So what was Jesus implying here?
A: He was God!

Those poor old Pharisees – he was really rubbing it in now. First he threw down the gauntlet by healing the leper, now he was forgiving sins!

Yet they were ordered just to observe him, not to interact with him. How agitated they must have been.

(Read Luke 5:21.)

They knew their sculptures and knew exactly what Jesus was demonstrating here.

(Read Luke 5:22.)

And Jesus knew what they knew!

(Read Luke 5:23.)

*(Write down the two phrases: "**Your sins are forgiven**" and "**get up and walk**".)*

Q: What is the easiest of these to say and why?
A: It was easier to say the first because it requires no physical evidence.
Q: If Jesus had just said this and had done nothing else what would the reaction have been?
A: They would have felt justified in calling him a blasphemer, because he'd offered no proof.

(Read Luke 5:24–25.)

So he backed up his words by making a proclamation:

"To prove that I can forgive sins I will heal this man."

It could still have gone wrong at that point – the man might have stayed unhealed. In which case the Pharisees would have been justified in calling him a blasphemer.

But the man was healed. The healing was not **just** to benefit the man, but to add weight to his words that he, as the Messiah (Christ), had the power to forgive sins.

And they were **very** impressed.

(Read Luke 5:26.)

Everyone was impressed and gave praise to God. They knew what they saw and what it meant. Jesus was proclaiming himself the Christ and was backing this up with evidence.

Discussion

So everyone was impressed and filled with awe. Yet most eventually turned away from him. If you had been there would you also have been impressed? If so, think about what subsequently happened. Why do you think that he was never really accepted by the religious authorities, culminating with his crucifixion by the Romans?

Prayer

Father, we thank you for this story. We thank you that you gave Jesus the power to forgive sins. We also thank you that even now, 2000 years later, you still forgive our sins. We ask you now to search our hearts, show us where we've gone wrong and to offer us your forgiveness for these sins.

Useful resources

http://www.77talksforteens.com/talk68.htm

69
A Day in the Life of Jesus: the Calling of Levi

Theme

An examination of Luke 5:27–32.

Preparation

Bibles for all, OHP/flip chart.

Presentation

We saw Jesus alert the religious authorities through his healing of the leper, causing them to send spies to follow him. These spies saw him heal the paralytic and also forgive his sins. They now had sufficient evidence that Jesus claimed to be Messiah in his actions as well as his words.

Q: What is a pariah?
A: (Not a high-flying parrot.) It's someone generally hated in society.
Q: Think of examples.
A: Lawyers, politicians, dentists . . . etc.

The one I'm looking for is the **tax man**.

In Jesus' day these were the pariahs. They were off-limits to other Jews, because their job was to collect money from their fellow Jews, to give to the Romans.

They were "one of us" through birth, but **not** "one of us" through what they did. They were deeply unpopular and were avoided at all costs, socially speaking.

They were particularly hated because they became rich at the expense of their fellow Jews, because of the enormous commissions they were able to earn – these days we'd be looking at Stock Market traders.

Religious authorities also hated them and classed them in the same group as prostitutes – avoid at all costs! Or else!

Now there were tax men and tax men. Some were the common-or-garden Inland Revenue types; others were the most hated and greedy custom officials – the equivalent of "Customs and Excise". These were **particularly** hated.

So, with this pretty picture painted, let's meet one of these customs officials.

(Read Luke 5:27–28.)

Levi (or **Matthew** – he of Gospel-writing fame) was a tax man.

Q: What was the cost of his decision to follow Jesus?
A: He gave up everything – particularly a well-off lifestyle.
Q: What would the other disciples think of this?
A: With suspicion – he was the first disciple coming from a hated profession, so life was not going to be easy for him.

So Levi was born again. And he thought he'd throw a birthday party.

(Read Luke 5:29.)

Q: And who were invited? *(Also read Mark 2:15.)*
A: Other tax collectors and sinners – these would be prostitutes, adulterers, robbers, etc. – some would call them "scum of the earth". These would be the only people **allowed** to associate with Levi. Also there were Jesus and his followers.

Discussion

So, just as Jesus mixed freely with "sinners", what does this tell us about who we should mix with?

Presentation

(Read Luke 5:30.)

Q: And who else had turned up?
A: Pharisees and teachers of the law.
Q: Why do you think they were there?
A: They were following Jesus around, to find fault in him.

They asked him why he had broken their religious rules by associating with these people.

(Read Luke 5:31–32.)

Jesus responds with two statements *(write on board)*.

• It is the sick that need healing, not the healthy.
• I have come for these "sick" ones – the sinners you see around you.

It is interesting to note that these Pharisees and religious leaders were now talking to him and questioning him. Alerted by his healing of the leper and having observed him in silence healing the paralytic, they were now free, according to the instructions they had been given, to voice their objections.

Q: Who was Jesus most concerned about in this gathering?
A: The "sinners" – tax men, prostitutes, etc.
Q: Why wasn't he so interested in the Pharisees and religious leaders?
A: Because they considered themselves "righteous".

Discussion

The nature of "righteousness". This word literally means "right behaviour" and "right standing" and the usual meaning is concerned with one's relationship with God.

Do you think Jesus considered the Pharisees righteous? (*Read Matthew 6:1–5.*) Stress that he tended to view their righteousness as self-righteousness. Do many Christians that you know fall into this category?

Prayer

Father, help us to be real with you, to be Christians on the inside rather than show-offs on the outside. Though you want us to express our faith in deeds, let this not be in a spirit of self-righteousness. If we give to the needy, let it be in private. If we pray aloud, let it not just be to show our cleverness. Help us to be real witnesses to the life you are living in us, to those around us and let it always be to your glory.

Useful resources

http://www.77talksforteens.com/talk69.htm

70
A Day in the Life of Jesus: Fasting

Theme

An examination of Luke 5:33–39.

Preparation

Bibles for all, OHP/flip chart.

Presentation

We saw Jesus alert the religious authorities through his healing
of the leper, causing them to send spies to follow him. These
spies saw him heal the paralytic and also forgive his sins and
now have sufficient evidence that Jesus claimed to be Messiah
in his actions as well as his words. By associating with sinners
Jesus had also stated that he has come for the "sinners" and
that he has no time for the "self righteous".

Q: What is more important: the birth of Jesus or Christmas
   presents?
A: The birth of Jesus (we hope!).

The birth of Jesus was a historical act. We commemorate this
at Christmas time, though, unfortunately, Christmas has
become a **tradition**, with lots of other extra bits thrown in – like
presents, trees, holly, etc. – that have nothing to do with the
actual story and don't focus our mind on what was really
important – the birth of Jesus!

Last week we left the Pharisees and religious teachers arguing
with Jesus. They are still arguing this week.

(Read Luke 5:33.)

Q: Why did these people fast?
A: Fasting is not part of Old Testament religious teaching. The only fast days mentioned are special occasions like the Day of Atonement. They fasted because this was in accordance with their own customs and traditions.

Pharisees fasted twice a week *(Luke 18:12)*. Fasting had become part of their tradition, rather than something God-ordained in Holy Scripture.

These traditions were called the Mishnah and had been formulated a couple of centuries earlier by learned rabbis. We see these traditions mentioned all through the Gospels as the "traditions of the elders".

(Read Luke 5:34–35.)

Q: Who is this bridegroom he is referring to?
A: Himself.

What he is saying is this:

"I'm here with you, don't you know what a favoured people you are? So why fast? You fast when I'm not here, but while I'm here – make the most of me!"

(Read Luke 5:35–36.)

What he is saying is this:

"Again, I am here and I am offering you something new and authentic. Stop following these 'traditions of the elders', they are man-made rules, but I am from God himself!"

(Read Luke 5:37–38.)

In those days they used goatskins to hold wine. As it ferments the wine expands and a new wineskin would stretch. But a used wineskin, that has already been stretched, would break.

So again Jesus tells them to follow him and not tradition. But he adds a warning.

(Read Luke 5:39.)

He warns against those stuck in the "old ways" and unwilling to change.

Q: What tone of voice would Jesus be using in this verse?
A: Mild sarcasm, resignation, sympathetic.

Discussion

How can we make sure that our faith and beliefs are fresh and that we don't sink into empty tradition? Can people list other church traditions that are not particularly helpful or useful? The key is always to look to biblical authenticity and not to writings by men.

Prayer

Father, help us to worship you in spirit and truth. Encourage us to question things and to turn to your word in the Bible. Give us boldness in proclaiming your truths, even if we are opposed by man-made traditions of others, but also give us love and patience in our dealings with others, always remembering that relationships with others are also important.

Useful resources

http://www.77talksforteens.com/talk70.htm

71
And the Greatest of These is . . .

Theme

A quick look at the Ten Commandments, concentrating on the spirit behind them rather than the externals.

Preparation

Make sure all have Bibles. Have OHP or flip chart prepared with list of the Ten Commandments (hidden from view), picture of a *mezuzah* (parchment fixed to Jewish doorposts) and *tefillin* (phylacteries – Matthew 23:5), copies of the Ten Commandments to give out afterwards.

Presentation

Everybody stand up on one leg, while I ask you all a question.

Can you name all the Kings and Queens of England from 1066 onwards? Without falling over?

Two problems, physical and mental – trying to stay balanced while you perform an impossible mental task.

There's a story of a famous Jewish teacher at the time of Jesus. His name was Rabbi Hillel. He was asked to teach the whole gist of the Jewish scriptures while standing on one leg. So he pulled up his tunic, lifted his sandalled foot and said the following. 'Don't do to others what you wouldn't want them to do to you. The rest is just commentary. Now go and study."

The point of this is that sometimes we look for detailed explanations, when an easy one will do. The learned Rabbi could have explained about Abraham and Isaac and Jacob, Moses and the Exodus, the giving of the Law, Joshua and the conquering of the land, as well as the 613 commandments within the Law – but his poor leg would have given way long before he finished. Instead he focused on the spirit behind the scriptures. That was all that was needed.

Jesus too was put on the spot one day. We read about it in Mark 12:28–31.

"One of the teachers of the Law came and heard them debating. Noticing that Jesus had given them a good answer, he asked him, 'Of all the commandments, which is the most important?' "

Again, a tricky question, but at least he didn't have to stand on one leg. Now Jesus had 613 to choose from, though ten of them, the Ten Commandments, were held up as being the most special and important.

A student was asked to list the Ten Commandments in any order. He wrote: 3, 6, 1, 8, 4, 5, 9, 2, 10, 7.

Now this is a test – do you know your Ten Commandments? Did you learn them in Sunday School and did they sink in? See how many you can remember.

The Ten Commandments: Exodus 20

1. You shall have no other Gods before me.
2. You shall not worship a false idol.
3. You shall not use God's name in vain (i.e. blaspheme).
4. Remember the Sabbath day.
5. Honour your parents.

6. Don't kill.
7. Don't commit adultery.
8. Don't steal.
9. Don't lie about your neighbours.
10. Don't lust after your neighbour's things (including his wife).

(Display these on the OHP/flip chart.)

Now, returning to our story, how did Jesus respond? Which one was he going to pick, since there were so many to choose from?

Let's put ourselves out of our suspense.

"The most important one", answered Jesus, "is this: 'Hear, O Israel, the Lord our God, the Lord is one. Love the Lord your God with all your heart and with all your soul and with all your mind and with all your strength.' The second is this: 'Love your neighbour as yourself.' There is no commandment greater than these."

Boy, was he clever, in this reply!

Rather than select one or two of the Ten Commandments, he did the same as our Rabbi Hillel. No, he didn't stand on one leg – his answer addressed the spirit **behind** the commandments.

In his first statement, he's basically combining the first four commandments *(indicate this on the OHP/flip chart)*.

If you love the Lord your God then you are going to want to . . . *(show first four Commandments – make point if necessary that keeping the Sabbath can be open to interpretation, but don't encourage discussions on this topic.)*

In his second statement, he's basically combining the next six commandments *(indicate this on the OHP/flip chart)*.

If you love your neighbour then you are going to want to . . . *(show last six Commandments)*.

So what he was doing was **summarising** the Ten Commandments. He was saying that all of the commandments are important, but let's concentrate on the spirit behind them – loving God and loving your neighbour.

But he was even cleverer than that, because his first statement was taken almost word for word from the most sacred scripture for Jewish people then and now. This is Deuteronomy 6:4, called the **Shema**, the Jewish confession of faith.

Shema: Deuteronomy 6:4–9. Hear, O Israel: The Lord our God, the Lord is one. Love the Lord your God with all your heart and with all your soul and with all your strength. These commandments that I give you today are to be upon your hearts. Impress them on your children. Talk about them when you sit at home and when you walk along the road, when you lie down and when you get up. Tie them as symbols on your hands and bind them on your foreheads. Write them on the door-frames of your houses and on your gates.

So in that one utterance he not only affirmed their accepted code of conduct, but also their confession of faith. He was telling them, "Hey, I'm not going against you here. Your scriptures are my scriptures."

He knew what he was doing . . . at all times.

Interestingly, even today Jewish people take the words of the Shema literally. They tie the words of the commandments on their hands and foreheads through the use of the **tefillin** (see

picture) and they write them on their door-frames through the
mezuzah.

Discussion

Ask whether the group think the Ten Commandments are still
relevant today. Do these rules still hold for us? What are the
easier ones, the first four or the last six? What are the
consequences for us not following the Ten Commandments?

Challenge

Take a copy of the Ten Commandments and keep them with
you all week (or at least one day). See how many you break
(nothing to be proud of, so don't see this as a competition!) and
report back next week to compare notes with others.

Useful resources

http://www.77talksforteens.com/talk71.htm

72
The Parable of the Man with a Litter of Puppies

Theme

We are surrounded by messages, coming at us from all angles. We suffer from information overload and are badly in need of a filtering system to separate the wheat from the chaff. Christians have such a filter, supplied by the Bible, under the control of the Holy Spirit. Looking at parables of Jesus in a modern context, we can explore some biblical truths.

Preparation

Flip chart with picture of cute little puppy. Perhaps a series of cartoon drawings of the four scenarios, if you (or someone you know) are suitably artistically talented. Bibles.

Presentation

Who likes little puppy dogs?

I knew a man who had a litter of puppies to give away.

The first he left in the middle of a busy road. Very soon a BMW came speeding along and flattened our poor little puppy.

The second he gave to a family of dubious background. They played with it for a bit but they soon got bored. They neglected the poor puppy, and left it in a shed without food and water. It soon died.

The third he let loose in the woods, where it joined the ranks of the other strays, living for scraps and fending for itself. It had a short unproductive life.

The fourth he gave to a good home, where it was loved and cherished and lived to a good old age, giving comfort to three generations.

Does the story remind you of anything? Does it ring a bell?

Picture the scene. A man stands in a boat near the shores of a lake. Facing him is a huge crowd of hundreds of people.

(Read Matthew 13:3–9: The Parable of the Sower.)

This is a **parable**.

Q: You've heard of the word, but what actually does it mean?
A: An everyday story that contains a spiritual truth.

We've all heard stories before and they all convey some sort of message. But how many of them contain spiritual truths?

Discussion

Explore the messages in the following stories: Harry Potter (witchcraft is cool?), Star Wars (good versus evil), the films of Quentin Tarantino (violence is exciting).

Presentation

Let's examine the spiritual truths of this parable. A man sows some seed.

Some seed fell on the path and was eaten by birds **or** one puppy was left on a path and was squished by a BMW.

Explanation: Some hear the message about Jesus but don't understand it and the Devil just snatches it away before "the light goes on". The message goes in one ear – provokes an immediate response – then out the other one! In this category could fit those people who are "converted" at large rallies, or in emotionally-charged meetings, but soon fall away.

Other seed fell in rocky places with shallow soil, where the shoots sprang up quickly but, because there were no roots, withered in the sun **or** one puppy was given "as a Christmas present" to a family who quickly got bored of it and neglected it, until it died.

Explanation: some hear the message about Jesus and receive it with joy but, when times get tough, find that there is no real grounding in the faith and they fall away. These will be people who haven't taken time to learn and grow in the faith (of course, no one here would fall into this category!) and, when they suffer a setback, turn their back on God.

Other seed fell on thorns which choked the plants **or** one puppy was left to fend for itself as a stray.

Explanation: some hear the message about Jesus but get choked up with the things of this world and what it has to offer. These end up being of no use at all to Jesus. These will be Christians who are Christians "in name only". They pay lip service, go to church on Sunday, but don't live productive Christian lives as Jesus would want for them. There are a lot of these in the church.

The other seeds fell on good soil and was the only seed to produce a decent crop **or** one puppy was given to a good home and was able to live a full productive life.

Explanation: some hear the message about Jesus and receive it willingly and understand it. These are the only really productive Christians. Can we count ourselves in this category?

Challenge

Look again at the Parable of the Sower and see if they can come up with a better modern-day equivalent than "The Parable of the man with the litter of puppies". If anyone does, then promise to send it to the publisher on the website, to be included in the discussion forum. What they will probably understand was that the content and structure of Jesus' parable just can't be bettered – it was the perfect explanation of a difficult truth in a way that first-century Jews could understand.

Discussion

Have a look at the other parables of Jesus and see if they can come up with modern-day equivalents. Good examples could be The Lost Sheep (Matthew 28:12–14), The Hidden Treasure (Matthew 13:44) and The Mustard Seed (Matthew 13:31).

Useful resources

http://www.77talksforteens.com/talk72.htm

73
Three Days of Destiny.
Day 1: The Trial

Theme

A dramatisation of the trial of Jesus, combining the facts from all the Gospels. The material is designed to be read out, with occasional pauses for teaching points and discussions. Note that the narrative is not exhaustive, but covers the key points.

Preparation

Photocopies of the script.

Presentation

(Read John 18:1–14.)

ANNAS: So you're the rabbi they're all talking about? The one who claims to be Messiah? Tell me again of your teachings.

JESUS: You all have heard my teachings. You know who I am, and what I represent, so why ask me again? If you're not sure, why not ask those who have already heard me?

NARRATOR: One of the guards slapped him and spoke to him.

GUARD: Don't speak in that way to your betters.

JESUS: If I have said anything wrong, tell everyone here what it was. But if I am right in what I have said, why do you hit me?

NARRATOR: Jesus was then taken to Caiaphas, the High Priest, where he was also faced by chief priests, teachers of the Law and elders. They had been

	unsuccessfully trying to find some false evidence against Jesus, so that he could be sentenced to death. Many witnesses came forward, but their stories didn't agree.
CAIAPHAS:	In the name of the living God I now put you on oath: tell us if you are the Messiah, the Son of God.
JESUS:	It is as you say. But I tell all of you: from this time on you will see the Son of Man sitting on the right of the Almighty and coming on the clouds of heaven!
CAIAPHAS:	Blasphemy! We don't need any more witnesses! You have just heard his blasphemy! What do you think?
ELDER:	He is guilty and must die!

Discussion

So the basis of his death sentence was blasphemy. They forced him to confess that he was the Son of God, a sin that, under Jewish law, was punishable by death. Even though he had done so much over the past three years to demonstrate that he **was** the Messiah, the Son of God. Why were they so unwilling to believe his claims?

Presentation

NARRATOR:	The guards blindfolded him and led him away. Some of them spat at him, others hit him and mocked him. They put him in chains and led him to Pilate, the Roman governor.
ELDER:	We caught this man telling people not to pay their taxes and also claiming to be our Messiah.
PILATE:	Are you the King of the Jews?
JESUS:	Does this question come from you or have others told you about me?

PILATE: Do you think I am a Jew? It was your own people and the chief priests who handed you over to me. What have you done?

JESUS: My kingdom doesn't belong to this world. If it did, my followers would fight to keep me from being handed over to the Jewish authorities. No, my kingdom doesn't belong here!

PILATE: Are you a king, then?

JESUS: You say that I'm a king. I was born and came into the world for this one purpose to speak about the truth. Whoever belongs to the truth listens to me.

PILATE: And what is truth?

NARRATOR: At that Jesus said no more. He had said enough.

PILATE: I find no reason to condemn this man.

ELDER: His teaching is starting a riot among the people all through Judea. He began in Galilee and now he's come here.

PILATE: I haven't found him guilty of any of the crimes you accuse him of. I'll have him whipped and let him go.

NARRATOR: It was pointed out to Pilate that, as it was Passover, it was customary to set free any one prisoner that the crowd asked for. The crowd had been manipulated by the chief priests so that another prisoner, the violent Barabbas, would be the one to be freed.

PILATE: Which one should go free?

CROWD: Barabbas!

PILATE: What about Jesus, the so-called Messiah?

CROWD: Crucify him!

PILATE: But what crime has he committed?

CROWD: Crucify him!

NARRATOR: So Barabbas was set free and Pilate had Jesus whipped, then handed over to be crucified.

Discussion

So who was to blame for his death? *(Read Matthew 26:56, Mark 10:33–34, Luke 23:34.)* The key is to stress that at all times he was master of his own destiny and that he was "born to die".

Useful resources

http://www.77talksforteens.com/talk73.htm

74
Three Days of Destiny.
Day 2: The Crucifixion

Theme

A dramatisation of the crucifixion of Jesus, combining the facts from all the Gospels. The material is designed to be read out, with occasional pauses for teaching points and discussions. Note that the narrative is not exhaustive, but covers the key points.

Preparation

Photocopies of the script.

Presentation

NARRATOR: Pontius Pilate had Jesus stripped and they put a scarlet robe on him, as well as a crown of thorns. They spat, jeered at him and mocked him, then led him out to be crucified. He was led to Golgotha, "the place of the skull", the place of execution.

NARRATOR: At Golgotha he was offered wine mixed with myrrh. He refused it.

SOLDIER: Save yourself if you're the King of the Jews!

NARRATOR: He was crucified and the soldiers divided his clothes among them by throwing dice. It was nine o'clock in the morning.

JESUS: Forgive them, Father! They don't know what they're doing.

SOLDIER: They say he's their king. Pilate told us to put this sign over his head – "This is Jesus – King of the Jews".

Discussion

Why did Pilate want this sign placed over his head (John 19:19–22)? What did this say to the Jewish religious authorities?

Presentation

NARRATOR:	Two others, both criminals, were crucified, on each side of him.
CRIMINAL 1:	Aren't you the Messiah? Save yourself and us!
CRIMINAL 2:	Don't you fear God? You received the same sentence he did. Ours is only right. We're getting what we deserve for what we did; but he hasn't done any wrong. Remember me, Jesus, when you come as King!
JESUS:	I promise you that today you'll be in paradise with me.
JEWISH PERSON:	You were going to tear down the temple and build it up again in three days! Save yourself if you're God's Son! Come on down from the cross!
CHIEF PRIEST:	He saved others, but he can't save himself! Isn't he the King of Israel? If he comes down off the cross now, we'll believe in him! He trusts in God and claims to be God's Son. Well, then, let's see if God wants to save him now!
NARRATOR:	Standing close by were the apostle John, Jesus' mother, his aunt and Mary of Magdalene.
JESUS:	Mother! John is your son now. John, look after my mother as if she were your mother.
NARRATOR:	At noon darkness came and the curtain hanging in the temple was torn in two. The darkness lasted for three hours.
JESUS:	My God, my God, why did you abandon me?

JEWISH PERSON: He's calling for Elijah! Let's see if Elijah is coming to save him!

JESUS: I am thirsty.

NARRATOR: Someone soaked a sponge in sour wine and tried to make him drink it.

JESUS: Father! Into your hands I place my spirit! It is finished!

NARRATOR: Jesus then gave a loud cry and breathed his last.

CHIEF SOLDIER: Come on, let's put him out of his misery. Break his legs.

SOLDIER   He is already dead, sir. I checked with my spear.

CHIEF SOLDIER: I've been watching him. He isn't like the others. He really was a good man. The Son of God, they say!

NARRATOR: When it was evening, a rich man, Joseph from Arimathea, a disciple of Jesus, arrived. He asked Pilate for the body of Jesus. Joseph took it, wrapped it in a new linen sheet, and placed it in his own tomb, which he had recently dug out of solid rock.

Discussion

Read Psalm 22:1–18 and discuss how this Psalm prophesied the events that have just occurred.

Useful resources

http://www.77talksforteens.com/talk74.htm

75
Three Days of Destiny.
Day 3: The Resurrection

Theme

A dramatisation of the resurrection of Jesus, combining the facts from all the gospels. The material is designed to be read out, with occasional pauses for teaching points and discussion. Note that the narrative is not exhaustive, but covers the key points.

Preparation

Photocopies of the script.

Presentation

(Read Matthew 27:57–66.)

NARRATOR: After the Sabbath, as Sunday morning was dawning, Mary Magdalene, Mary the mother of James, and Salome brought spices to go and anoint the body of Jesus.

MARY: Who will roll away the stone for us from the entrance to the tomb? It's a very large stone, after all.

NARRATOR: Suddenly there was a violent earthquake and when they got there they found that the stone had been rolled away.

GUARD 1: My knees are fair trembling.

GUARD 2: Mine too, I suggest we leg it.

NARRATOR: The guards were really scared. Mary stood crying outside the tomb. While she was still crying, she bent over and looked in the tomb and saw two angels there dressed in white, sitting where the body of Jesus had been, one at the head and the other at the feet.

ANGEL 1: Woman, why are you crying?

MARY: They have taken my Lord away, and I don't know where they have put him!

NARRATOR: Then she turned round and saw Jesus standing there; but she didn't know it was Jesus.

JESUS: Woman, why are you crying? Who are you looking for?

MARY: If you took him away, sir, tell me where you've put him, and I'll go and get him.

JESUS: Mary!

MARY: Teacher! It's you!

JESUS: Don't hold on to me, because I haven't yet gone back up to the Father. But go to my brothers and tell them that I'm returning to my Father and their Father, my God and their God.

NARRATOR: The other two women also entered the tomb and saw the angels.

ANGEL 1: You mustn't be afraid. I know you're looking for Jesus, who was crucified. He isn't here; he has been raised, just as he said. Come here and see the place where he was lying.

ANGEL 2: Why are you looking among the dead for one who is alive? He isn't here; he has been raised. Remember what he said to you while he was in Galilee: "The Son of Man must be handed over to sinners, be crucified, and three days later rise to life."

ANGEL 1: Go quickly now, and tell his disciples, "He has been raised from death, and now he is going to Galilee ahead of you; there you will see him!" Remember what I have told you.

NARRATOR: They left the tomb in a hurry, afraid and yet filled

with joy, and ran to tell his disciples. Suddenly
Jesus met them.

JESUS: Peace be with you.

NARRATOR: They came up to him, took hold of his feet, and
worshipped him.

JESUS: Don't be afraid. Go and tell my brothers to go to
Galilee, and they'll see me there.

NARRATOR: The women arrived at the apostles' house and told
them everything.

APOSTLE 1:   Nonsense!

APOSTLE 2:   Poppycock!

PETER: I'm going to find out myself.

JOHN: Me too!

NARRATOR: Peter got up and ran to the tomb. John ran faster
than Peter and reached the tomb first. He bent
over and saw the linen wrappings, but he didn't go
in. Behind him came Peter, and he went straight
into the tomb and saw the linen wrappings lying
there. Then John also went in; he saw and believed.
Then the disciples went back home amazed at
what had happened.

Discussion

Why do you think Peter and John had to go and see for
themselves? Why didn't the other disciples also go with
them?

Presentation

NARRATOR: Meanwhile the guards went back to the city and
told the chief priests everything that had
happened. The chief priests met with the elders
and made their plan; they gave a large sum of
money to the soldiers and said:

CHIEF PRIEST: You are to say that his disciples came during the

	night and stole his body while you were asleep. And if the Governor should hear of this, we'll convince him that you're innocent, and you'll have nothing to worry about.
GUARD 1:	And why should we do this?
CHIEF PRIEST:	Take this large amount of money.
GUARD 1:	That should do nicely.
NARRATOR:	Meanwhile, it was late that Sunday evening, and the disciples were gathered together behind locked doors, because they were afraid of the Jewish authorities. Then Jesus came and stood among them.
JESUS:	Peace be with you.
NARRATOR:	After saying this, he showed them his hands and his side. The disciples were filled with joy at seeing the Lord.
JESUS:	Peace be with you. As the Father sent me, so I send you. Receive the Holy Spirit. If you forgive people's sins, they are forgiven; if you do not forgive them, they are not forgiven.
NARRATOR:	One of the disciples, Thomas, wasn't with them when Jesus came.
PETER:	We have seen the Lord!
THOMAS:	Unless I see the scars of the nails in his hands and put my finger on those scars and my hand in his side, I won't believe it.
NARRATOR:	A week later the disciples were together again indoors, and Thomas was with them. The doors were locked, but Jesus came and stood among them.
JESUS:	Peace be with you.
NARRATOR:	Then Jesus turned to Thomas.
JESUS:	Put your finger here, and look at my hands; then stretch out your hand and put it in my side. Stop your doubting, and believe!
THOMAS:	My Lord and my God!

JESUS: Do you believe because you see me? How happy are those who believe without seeing me!

NARRATOR: Later the eleven disciples went to the hill in Galilee where Jesus had told them to go. Jesus appeared to them and they worshipped him, even though some of them doubted.

JESUS: I have been given all authority in heaven and on earth. Go, then, to all peoples everywhere and make them my disciples: baptise them in the name of the Father, the Son and the Holy Spirit, and teach them to obey everything I have commanded you. And I will be with you always, to the end of the age.

Discussion

Why did Thomas not believe at first? Didn't he trust his friends? What can we learn from Jesus's comments to Thomas?

Useful resources

http://www.77talksforteens.com/talk75.htm

76
Magical Spiritual Tour

Theme

A short Bible study that cunningly ties together three Bible passages and shows the Bible as internally consistent.

Preparation

OHP/flip chart.

Presentation

The Bible can be exciting, but never more exciting as when it spills its secrets.

I've said my piece, now I'm going to back it up.

(Read Mark 11:15–18.)

Jesus and the Moneychangers. You know the story, you may have read it a few times.

Q: There's something that stands out from this story, something that is easily missed, but something quite awesome. What is it? *(Read story again.)*
A: Verse 18: ". . . the whole crowd was amazed at his teaching."
Q: What was so amazing about this teaching? The clue is in what he said, rather than what he did.
A: *(Read Verse 17.)*

What he said here was so significant that we read that the chief priests and the teachers were afraid of him.

Why should they be afraid – afraid enough to want to kill him?

The crowd was amazed. Are we?

Here's a clue: Jews of that day were very knowledgeable about their scripture – our Old Testament (the New Testament hadn't been written yet). They knew their scripture like we know our Simpsons (American cartoon variety)!

When Jesus quoted scripture, they knew **exactly** what he was talking about.

Let's look at the two things he said:

"My temple will be called a house of prayer for the people of all nations." *(Write on chart.)*

(Read Isaiah 56:7.)

This is where it came from and the people there knew it – especially the priests!

He was referring to the true purpose of the temple in the sight of God.

But now the punchline.

"But you have turned it into a hideout for thieves!"

(Write on chart.)

(Read Jeremiah 7:1–15.)

So here Jeremiah too was preaching in the temple, hundreds of years before Jesus. He is reading out a list of sins of the people, but he also tells them that, if they change their ways, they will be saved and allowed to live there.

(Read verse 11 again and point to chart.)

Q: Then he gives a warning. What is it?
A: Remember Shiloh – sounds like a cowboy film.

Now, these days, if we want to give a warning I could say something like:

"Remember Hiroshima" or "Remember Vietnam" or "Remember Bill Clinton" – each one conjures up an image that would serve as a warning to a group of people. *(Ask for further examples.)*

But "Remember Shiloh"? *(Write on chart.)*

Did they know what he meant? They sure did!

(Read 1 Samuel 4:1–11.)

(Write on chart.)

Shiloh was ingrained in the Jewish mind in the same way as Dresden or Vietnam could be for the older generation in England or the USA today. It wasn't a happy memory.

In this story they were reminded of the corrupt sons of Eli the priest, who allowed the Ark of the Covenant to be moved, despite God's instructions, resulting in a massive defeat by the Philistines, the death of these sons and the capture of the Ark.

This was God pronouncing judgement on corrupt priests.

So, when Jesus said, "My temple will be called a house of prayer for the people of all nations, but you have turned it into a hideout for thieves," he was combining these three verses from Isaiah, Jeremiah and 1 Samuel and what he was really saying was this:

"Because you priests are so corrupt I am going to destroy this temple as I did at Shiloh, when the Ark of the Covenant was captured, and put an end to your priesthood."

No wonder they wanted to kill him!

It was just 40 years later that the temple was destroyed and the priesthood was brought to an end.

Discussion

You may need to go through this lesson again to highlight key points. It is designed to show the consistency of scripture and how Jesus can use scripture to drive home key points. It also shows that he was a prophet with 100% accuracy!

Useful resources

http://www.77talksforteens.com/talk76.htm

77
It's Raining Men, Praise the Lord!

Theme

A word study on the much-used and maligned Hebrew word, "Hallelujah".

Preparation

OHP/flip chart. Guitar (and guitarist) – selection of songs featuring the word "Hallelujah". See website for list.

Presentation

There's a song that occasionally hits the charts that has been performed by such varied acts as the Weather Girls and Geri Halliwell.

It starts . . . "It's raining men".

(Encourage them to sing the next word.)

Hallelujah!

How on earth did this Hebrew word get from the pages of the Bible to the lips of a Spice Girl?

It's a much-used word. Sometimes when a word is used a lot, it can lose its original meaning.

Today we are going to look at its original meaning.

Q: Does anyone know exactly what this word means?
A: Praise God.

Pretty obvious really.

(Write on chart "HALLELU YAH".)

These are the two Hebrew words that are added together.

The first word comes from **hallel,** the Hebrew word for **praise**.

A whole section of the Psalms – Psalms 113 to 118 – are called "The Hallel". In fact, if we read the first word of Psalm 113, we find that it is . . . **HALLELUJAH** – Praise the Lord.

At the end of Jesus' Last Supper, we read in Matthew 26:30 that they sang a hymn before travelling to the Mount of Olives. What they sang was "The Hallel".

The second word is **YAH**, which tells us who we are praising.

When God is spoken of in the Old Testament, the word used is "Yahweh" – **Yah** is a shortened form.

But what does the word "hallelujah" **really** mean?

It's an instruction. It's telling us to praise God – it's not telling us to repeat the word hallelujah 500 times!

Imagine you're in a TV lounge. The TV is switched off and everyone is calling out the words, "Turn on the TV!" The words alone won't get the job done, someone has to physically make the effort to flip that switch!

It's the same with praising God. Singing hallelujah umpteen times is **not** praising God, it's **talking about** praising God, it's telling us to praise God, it's encouraging us to praise God. Until someone does something about it, God is going to stay . . . unpraised (and no doubt bored to tears!).

Can you imagine what it would be like in a prayer meeting if all everyone said was "Let's pray" and nothing else?

So, when we get together, the word "hallelujah" really should be said just once and the rest of the time should be spent doing the praising, in our own words!

Activity

Spend the rest of the time in worship, praising the Lord.

Useful resources

http://www.77talksforteens.com/talk77.htm